QUEENS OF THE RESISTANCE:
NANCY PELOSI

QUEENS OF THE RESISTANCE:

NANCY PELOSI

———————★———————

The Life, Times, and Rise of
Madam Speaker, aka the *OG*

———————★———————

BRENDA JONES AND KRISHAN TROTMAN

PLUME

PLUME

An imprint of Penguin Random House LLC
penguinrandomhouse.com

Copyright © 2020 by Brenda Jones and Krishan Trotman

Penguin supports copyright. Copyright fuels creativity, encourages diverse
voices, promotes free speech, and creates a vibrant culture. Thank you for
buying an authorized edition of this book and for complying with
copyright laws by not reproducing, scanning, or distributing any part of it
in any form without permission. You are supporting writers and allowing
Penguin to continue to publish books for every reader.

Plume is a registered trademark and its colophon is a trademark of
Penguin Random House LLC.

Illustrations by Jonell Joshua
Interior Hand Lettering by Jonell Joshua and Dominique Jones

LIBRARY OF CONGRESS CATALOGING-IN-PUBLICATION DATA
has been applied for.

ISBN 9780593189887 (POB)
ISBN 9780593189924 (ebook)

Printed in the United States of America
1   3   5   7   9   10   8   6   4   2

BOOK DESIGN BY TIFFANY ESTREICHER

For Nancy Pelosi,
and all the Queens of the Resistance reading this

CONTENTS

You wanna be this Queen B,
But ya can't be
That's why you're mad at me.
—Lil' Kim, "Big Momma Thang"

INTRODUCTION:
THE QUEENS OF THE
RESISTANCE SERIES

Dear Sis,

The Queens of the Resistance is a series that celebrates the life and times as well as the lessons and rise of our favorite sheroes and Queen Bees of politics. It's a celebration of the *boss*, the loud in their demands, and a rebellion against the long and tired patriarchy. They are the shining light and new face of the US government. The idea for the series began to germinate in 2016. Hillary Clinton was in the presidential race. She was top dog, Grade A. She was supposed to go all the way as the first female president. She had done everything right. In the 1960s, she switched parties when the Civil Rights movement was demonstrating that changing allegiance wasn't about betting on the winner but believing in a different vision for America's future. She married one of the most capable politicians of the twentieth century, Bill Clinton, who would eventually appoint the first Black secretaries of commerce and labor and put women and minorities in many positions of power. She was considered most likely to be president when she gave a commencement speech during her graduation from Wellesley, then went on to graduate Yale Law at the head of her class. She was the first female partner of two law firms in Arkansas; First Lady of Arkansas; First Lady of the United States—but she didn't stop there. She became the first female US senator from New York, a seat that had positioned Robert Kennedy to run for president, and one of the first female secretaries of state. She was the first woman *ever* to be nominated by a major political party to run for president. Even the political machine was oiled and greased to work in her favor. She had been generally considered one of the most qualified people ever to run for president, even by her opponents, but with all that going for her, somehow, some way, she didn't make it. *sigh* You can't get more presidential than Hillary Clinton in 2016. She had it all, even the majority of popular votes in the 2016 election.

So what happened? Ha! Every woman knows what happened! Everybody laughed at her in 1995, when she appeared on the *Today* show and attributed the chop-down of her husband to a "vast right-wing conspiracy," but she was right. Who knew that while we were enjoying the moment, the wind beneath our wings after two terms with the first Black president, a time that had left us proximal to a variety of enjoyable mini multi-cultures—sushi, guacamole, break dancing—there was a group of malcontents intent on making America great again . . . "great" like the 1940s. And that meant forcing women back into the kitchen, padlocking the door, and throwing away the key. There'd be no need to vilify female candidates with memes, negative ads, and sucker punches like the opposition had to do to Hillary Clinton; the social stigma would do all the policing and policy work needed to keep women out of the ring and out of the way, so the boyz could rule, unchecked, unaccountable, and unrestrained. "Less for you, more for me" has been a natural law in a capitalist society. It means getting rid of competition by every means necessary—deportation, mass incarceration, legislation, deprivation, deconstruction, and divestment, to name a few. Our sister Hillary was a woman who fell in the crosshairs of a right-wing machine dead set against any diversion from its outrageous plan—to stop collective action and make sure politics bends only to its will, not the people's. It didn't matter that Hillary was the smartest, the most prepared, or the first in this or that. Merit's not the point; it's compliance that matters, and Hillary was just too damn smart, too capable, too talented, for her own good. She had a vast right-wing conspiracy working against her, and they won . . . temporarily.

And that's where this series begins. Queens of the Resistance is as much an ode to the women themselves as it is a celebration of a transcending political identity in America, unlike anything our history has ever shown us before.

With Love,
Brenda & Krishan

QUEENS OF THE RESISTANCE:
NANCY PELOSI

★ ★ ★ ★ ★ ★ ★ ★ ★ ★ ★ ★ ★ ★ ★

BORN

We predict that
this little lady will soon
be a "Queen" in her
own right.

—*THE GUIDE*, MARCH 28, 1941, ON PELOSI'S BIRTH

ALWAYS, ITALY ♥

Looks like a girl, but she's a flame
So bright, she could burn your eyes.
—Alicia Keys, "Girl on Fire"

*T*ip-tap-tip-tap-tippity-tap is the elegant sound of Speaker Pelosi's four-inch heels as she cuts a path through the marble-encrusted boys' club on Capitol Hill. When she wields the gavel, women around the country rejoice because she's the first woman yet to do so.

Walk softly and carry a big stick personifies this Madam Speaker, and, like Beyoncé, she's got the persuasion to build a nation. As Speaker, her job is an entirely different ball of wax that requires herding all the *cats* in Congress and gaining their fealty. King Arthur never had a bigger challenge. The Knights of the Round Table, fully clothed in armor and ready for battle, had nothing on Congress. Only a master could stand down the forces that have attempted to divide the country, and that she is. A youngblood would sweat and struggle against a McConnell or Trump, but OGs, they know the job, they made the ropes and built the ladders. Folks have come for Pelosi's head, but as an OG, she's been there, done that. In the name of justice, fair and square, there's no need for a showdown; when she's ready, she'll take you down.

She's a woman, unapologetically. Her presence behind the Speaker's rostrum is an eminent reminder that the old and tired guard, the cobwebbed patriarchy that has been Congress for ages, is a dying one. The Queens have arrived.

Always in full face and hair on *fleek*, her rep in the marble byways of Congress is the power broker and the *boss*. Her style is queenly and she emits light inside and outside of the House, always leading with strength, dignity, and a decidedly feminine panache. She holds her ambition close to the vest, but make no mistake about it, Speaker Pelosi gets sh*t done. She's the gloved hand of the Democratic Party, the enforcer of a smooth resistance, a one-woman political machine who knows all the shots that need to be called. Leadership—she was born for it. She's got she-power, hurrah, and you can find her at the head of it all.

THIS QUEEN, BORN Nancy D'Alesandro, was delivered unto us in Baltimore, on March 26, 1940, an Aries. When she was first introduced to the world, it seemed like destiny had already sent a message. "We predict that this little lady will soon be a 'Queen' in her own right" were the words in the local

Baltimore newspaper *The Guide* about a year after the birth of a girl, Little Nancy D'Alesandro. The headline read, "Prediction: D'Alesandro Will Find New Boss in First Daughter." It was an unwitting prophecy. Brown-haired with big hazelnut eyes, she was a crowned gift to her parents, Thomas D'Alesandro Jr. and Annunciata D'Alesandro. Finally, their first girl had arrived after five rough-and-tumble sons. Her mother exhaled; her father could weep. Here she was, the second-generation little lady to a big boss of Albemarle Street. *Hooray!*

But let's back up for a minute. Thomas "Tommaso" D'Alesandro Sr., her grandfather, had come to Baltimore from the majestic mountains and lakes of Abruzzo, Italy, where the aromas of mutton and pork, savory legumes, and handmade spaghetti alla chitarra reigned among charming medieval towns. For more than two hundred years Abruzzo had been producing some of the world's best pasta, and it had been home to Tommaso since he was born in 1903. When Tommaso arrived in the United States, it was in Baltimore's Little Italy that he settled. There was a growing community of Italians, where the smells of garlic, basil, and tomato could be caught among the wooden-clad halls and apartment doors. In the late nineteenth century, waves of Italians had immigrated to the area, which rests east of the Inner Harbor in the Patapsco River. At the time, the neighborhood was an enclave populated by other immigrant communities: the Irish, the Germans, and the Jews. A decade later the neighborhood would emerge and unveil itself as majority Italian American. (Those were the demographics at the time, but Maryland has cooked up more than good pasta; it has birthed Frederick Douglass, Thurgood Marshall, and, hello, Jada Pinkett Smith!)

Baltimore definitely wasn't the pristine landscape of the sun-splashed mountains of Abruzzo but, ultimately, culture is bound to the heart, home is in the spirit, and though the people of Baltimore's Little Italy would always be tied to the traditions and the ways of their ancestral home in the Old World, they were also wedded to the forces of democracy, and the collective American struggle against tyranny had become their struggle.

The closeness of the little row houses, side by side, brick on brick, held their families and their neighbors' families together; it was in this network of adults where their children were raised, protected, and disciplined, and each neighbor was accountable to the others. The men threw bocce balls on Saturdays and marched up the hill with their families every Sunday to kneel in prayer during mass at Saint Leo's Catholic Church. The procession was lined with women whose hair was *done*, baby—adorned and decadent under soft scarves as they sashayed with gloved hands on the arms of their men. There'd be a fleet of girls in fresh-cut dresses and boys in little tailored suits in tow. (This generation could school your generation in how to spell "haute couture," *okay?*)

Nancy's grandfather opened up a store and met her future grandmother, Maria Petronilla Foppiani, and they married and had thirteen children. (Pause: imagine having thirteen children.) Nancy's father, Thomas Jr., later known as Big Tommy, aka Old Tommy, aka Tommy the Elder despite being the second of his name, was born on Albemarle Street.

The first female Speaker of the House would also grow up at 245 Albemarle Street. Albemarle Street was the foundation, the birth, and the beginning of the dynasty, and later their stomping grounds for battle. One set of grandparents lived at 235 Albemarle and the other at 204; Aunt Jessie was at 314; and Aunt Mary lived just around the corner. Spike Lee would have loved to produce a film about that joint if it had been in Brooklyn. It was a fortress of the D'Alesandro empire, one of the fiercest families on the block, like the Jeffersons or the Waltons.

After getting into a fight at school one day when he was thirteen years old, Big Tommy decided not to go back. He began delivering newspapers to help his family of twelve brothers and sisters. It wasn't a hard-knock life, Jay-Z; leaving school at a young age wasn't uncommon, and many folks did so and had successful lives—but Big Tommy, the future politician, was a soul destined for success via an uncommon route.

Big Tommy had a career sooner than most; he started selling insurance door-to-door. As part of a big family, there was a real need to bring in dinero quickly. He was growing up in

Baltimore during the age of progressive politics, where businesses and corporations were getting fat and more industrialized while the lives of workers—the average American citizens—were becoming more impoverished and constricted. He knew their stories; as a young, buckskin insurance guy, he talked to everyone. These were the days before the advent of labor laws and the designated eight-hour workday that we actually bemoan today. Generations prior worked as many as ten to fourteen hours a day. The poor worked in unsafe, unsanitary conditions, but the bosses didn't care as long as they were making money. It was before mandatory lunch breaks were a rule of thumb, before sick and holiday leave were a talking point in politics. Nancy's dad witnessed activism in the labor movement, and the rise of progressive politicians who had begun to turn the tide for the working man. Coming from where he did, knowing who and what he knew, he wanted to help. Policy was the change-maker; he wanted in.

He was running around Baltimore collecting insurance dues for a paycheck of $5 per week, which, to be fair, was decent money for someone his age. After years of hard work, he eventually became a broker and opened his own agency. He was handsome and popular . . . and he could dance, which only made him more popular. He entered ballroom dancing competitions and won prizes and became sort of famous around town. He took business classes at Calvary Business School, but he secretly wanted to be a priest. All of this in one Italian waltz made Big Tommy a character with flair, a true peacock. And the political world wanted him.

Democratic Party leaders in the community noticed him—and named him an Election Day precinct runner. Many decades before the development of computers, the runner played a very important role, and actually still does today. Tommy would receive voter lists at designated points during Election Day from each precinct. Those lists verify the names of those who have voted. He would bring those lists to the party chair, who would compare them with lists of those eligible to vote, and then deploy resources to help get people out to the polls—an especially important strategy in areas within the precinct that were underperforming. Big Tommy quickly grasped the significance of counting votes. (I mean, with twelve siblings, he probably was the best at counting!) He witnessed firsthand the way that votes can alter people's lives, and the ways a party apparatus manages an election, all key factors in understanding the intricacies of politics.

All those years going door-to-door came in handy when he decided to run for public office: he called upon all of those neighbors he got to know as a teenager to secure his first election. Leveraging that strong community connection, he went out and raised five thousand signatures himself to qualify and then won. He was elected to Maryland's House of Delegates in 1926 at the young age of twenty-one and served for seven years.

He went on to win twenty-two elections in a row. After his time in the State House, he spent three years on the Baltimore City Council. Then he became a member of the Maryland delegation in the US House of Representatives and served for four consecutive terms. He later served as mayor of Baltimore for twelve years.

Some might see mayor as a step down from the US Congress, but D'Alesandro's interest was in serving his people on the local level. He had been elected to the Baltimore City Council during the height of the Great Depression, so finding a job was the overriding concern of most of his constituents. Then, starting in 1939, when Representative D'Alesandro rode the train from Baltimore to DC, people would talk to him during the whole journey about their concerns and needs. Federal legislators do not have the power that mayors do to hire and fire city officials. Big Tommy knew he could do more to support the day-to-day lives of individual Baltimoreans as mayor than he could in Congress. "I'm a *paisan*," the mayor would say. "These are my people. This is where I belong."

BY THE TIME Little Nancy was born, her father was a notable US Representative from Maryland who had been running and winning elections for sixteen years, and that's why she made headlines. The day she was born, Big Tommy found himself on the House floor in Washington, working to win votes for a

BRENDA JONES and KRISHAN TROTMAN

Democratic bill. When word arrived that Annunciata was about to give birth, Thomas made sure his vote would not be nullified if he were absent. (Back in the day, childbearing was between a woman and her doctor. Paternity leave? Ha, God forbid! Plus, with all that goes on during labor? No, thanks; the men were to wait outside. It was common for Dad to be at the office until after the drama unfolded.) Then he rushed off to the hospital to meet his new daughter. Nancy would be the only girl among five older brothers in a house steeped in politics.

Inside a traditional Italian family of five boys, Little Nancy would offer a new wrinkle. It would be Nancy, and not her brothers, who would become the heir apparent, the extension of her father's lineage who would eventually surpass him and distinguish herself as a leader in politics.

A lot of that energy and expertise would come from her upbringing, sis. The D'Alesandro household, a three-story row house that doubled as their family home and her father's office, was run like a state office. Sound the doorbell. Their doors would open to the public at ten A.M., and each child had a designated time to man the front door. Little Nancy and her brothers would be allotted different jobs and responsibilities. Their little hands stuffed envelopes, answered the phones, and served as Daddy's helpers to the daily flow of constituents. "If you entered the house, it was always campaign time, and if you went into the living room, it was always constituent

Don't characterize
the strength that
I bring...

time," Nancy later said; it was only on Christmas or Easter when you "were not given a placard or a bumper sticker or a brochure to distribute." There was a file full of community favors that the children managed daily—they also kept track of how many votes from every part of the community they had, or needed to secure, to win the next election. This was all lingo that the D'Alesandro kids were rapping right out of the womb. Big Tommy would frequently call out, "Make sure you have the votes!" And those little legs would race to the box and get to countin'. People were always stopping by. Little Nancy grew up understanding politics, not as an elite measure of status or power but as a very personal way to serve the people around her.

Sis, politics in the D'Alesandro household was not some hot-air-balloon artifice, flying way over the heads of average citizens. No one had to wrap their minds around Bitcoins. It was about making sure that the people in the community had jobs and childcare. The immigrant woman whose husband had gotten into trouble with the law and who didn't know where to turn for help? She could find support at the D'Alesandros'. The worker who had lost his job but couldn't afford an attorney? He could go to 245 Albemarle Street for some guidance. The community members needed a public official who cared about them, their businesses, their homes. It sounds like it could be tough coming of age in this family, exposed to the real ways of responsibility, but in actuality the home was often glowing with love due to all the good that took place there. The love for the people. The lather of determination.

Thomas D'Alesandro knew that the key to political clout was staying connected to the people who elected him, hearing their concerns, and translating those needs into visible results. He worked in Washington, but unlike most representatives, he could return to his district every night, and the people of Little Italy always knew where to find him.

BIG NANCY

B ig Tommy wasn't the only political big fish and role model in the house. Nancy's mother, Annunciata (who sometimes went by the Americanized name Nancy), was the queen of their chamber, the backbone in any chaos, the one who could *make it happen*. No matter what *it* was. She was born in Naples, Italy, but moved to Albemarle Street when she was an infant. At one point her family moved back to Italy and later returned to Albemarle Street, moving just across the street and a few doors down from the home that would become hers and Tommy's years later.

She had once had her own career, after graduating from the Institute of Notre Dame, as Baltimore's first female auctioneer. Girl, it was a position unheard-of for a woman in the 1920s, but she was so good that her employer wanted to get her a national certificate. When she was asked to relocate to

New York, though, she declined—maybe in another era she could have followed that dream, but at the time, family came first, so she needed to remain close to them.

Nancy was nineteen years old and Big Tommy was twenty-five when they got married. She had known this guy since they were kids, with marbles and board games, but now before her was a young, handsome statesman with dreams and a heart as big as her own, and with ambition to match.

While he exemplified more of the brash, independent Americano personality, she represented a kind of European elegance. She spoke perfect Italian, unlike her husband. She always stepped out with an impeccable appearance—dripping in sophistication from head to toe, baby—and with a brain as sharp as a tack.

As the mother of 245 Albemarle Street, she was the queen. Little Nancy's father taught her invaluable principles that would be like a flagpole in her career, such as "always keep the friendship in your voice," which is why the Speaker can hold a friendly smile even when under the gaze of a pack of crouching tigers mad about the president's impeachment.

But it was Nancy's mother who taught her how to lead and manage a team, honey. This woman could multitask and strategize like a subway-car dancer, with dozens of moves, circumstances, and human beings all at once.

She had been pregnant throughout many of her husband's campaigns, but that never stopped her. Big Nancy had two maids who helped clean, and she did all the cooking. After she made breakfast and her husband left for work and her children went off to school, the doors of their row house were flung open to the world. It was Annunciata, of course, who organized those shifts the children would take when the doors opened at ten A.M. Big Nancy once told a *Baltimore Sun* reporter that a neighborhood boy had once asked to volunteer to answer the phones at their Albemarle home. "The phone was always ringing," she said in the 1985 interview, "and the kids were always running around." The young volunteer got his fill of the work—she joked that he left after half a day because he couldn't hack it. It was hard work, but good work. Thomas III, Nancy's brother, later recalled that when he was seven or eight, people formed lines at his house that wound around the block, asking for assistance. By the time she was in grade school, Nancy herself later said, "I knew how to answer the phone and to tell people where to go if they needed a bed in a city hospital, or where to call to get into a housing project."

Food was easy to come by at Big Nancy's castle—Annunciata often made big pots of spaghetti for hungry constituents. Aunts would come by to assist with platters of lasagna and ravioli. The traditions of Little Italy welcomed any neighbor or friend to take a seat at the table. With an open-door policy engineered by Big Nancy herself, she merged culture, community, and child-rearing with her husband's political life. She embraced her responsibility as a mother and daughter of Christ with full fervor, and she used her ingenuity to satisfy everything required of her. Thomas III—who would also become mayor of Baltimore—once said that had Annunciata been born today, the sky would have been the limit for her. Instead, she had to face the limitations of femininity imposed by a fairly rigid traditional Italian family structure and the expectations of an American society that demanded a woman concentrate all her efforts in the home. But Big Nancy met every demand by making her home a base of power.

While Big Tommy was away in Washington negotiating with committee chairs, House and Senate minority and majority leaders, and even presidents, Big Nancy was in their living room in Baltimore, managing his relationships with his constituents at home. This part of the job is fundamental to a successful political career. After all, it's voters who put politicians in office.

Big Nancy would recruit other queens of the neighborhood, who understood their power as well and what was at stake, and they'd get into formation—knocking on doors, handing out flyers, doing what they could—and they'd win! Women are the linchpin, the door that unlocks all political success. (Hello, many of them have birthed the voting population. Who has more influence than *yo mama*?!) Women in general are more likely to turn up and turn out at the polls than their counterparts. If women were to decide to stay home, to give their cat a haircut instead on Election Day, it would be all over, honey. Without our support and our muscles, a politician's ambitions are just pipe dreams.

It was Nancy D'Alesandro who understood the intricate design of the community and how one human problem connected to an entire family dynamic. She was the one who met the people every day, who held their hands, who heard their problems, who gave them handkerchiefs when they broke down in tears. She was the one who empathized, who directed them to places when they needed help, who knew them all by name, their parents and their children, who understood their motivations and their weaknesses, who could track the wax and wane of neighborhood grievances.

With all of this know-how, she couched her motivation in her husband's success. She said that her actions were "what Tommy wanted," and she used her capacity and her intellect to execute what his ambition required. In fact, in his campaign to become governor in 1954, some complications outside of his control arose—though he had a good chance of winning the election, suddenly he was wrongfully embroiled in a scandal (allegations of taking undisclosed donations from a shady local character, of which he was later exonerated). Even though Tommy hadn't done anything wrong, Nancy saw the writing on the wall and told her husband the other politicians had decided to sacrifice him. The drama put him in a position where members of the state party wanted him to leave the race to make sure another Democrat won. With her community connections, she might have been able to help, and she knew it: "You should have come to me," she told him. He ended up withdrawing from the race and backing his primary opponent instead.

In many ways, young Nancy, though a daughter of a very successful politician from Maryland, actually was her mother's prodigy. Her mother was her greatest inspiration and mentor, who demonstrated a dynamic energy that her brothers would not be able to emulate: blending that feminine-coded power with pragmatism to navigate the echelons of power. Nancy absorbed her mother's instincts as "the real politician in the family," and that approach became her template to become the first woman Speaker of the House.

★ ★ ★ ★ ★ ★ ★ ★ ★ ★ ★

WOMAN

I never thought that
I would go from
the kitchen to the
Congress; that I would
go from homemaker
to House Speaker.
But that's what I did.

—NANCY PELOSI, MORGAN STATE UNIVERSITY
COMMENCEMENT ADDRESS, 2016

LIKE A PRAYER

I hear you call my name, and it feels like home.
—Madonna, "Like a Prayer"

L ittle Nancy attended high school at her mother's alma
mater, the Institute of Notre Dame, a Catholic private
all-girls school founded in 1847, while her brothers attended the neighborhood school. The founder of the Sisters
of Notre Dame was Saint Julie Billiart, who grew up poor
working in the fields of Cuvilly, France, in the mid–1700s, and
suffered twenty-two years of paralysis. She became a nun at
fourteen, the same age that Little Nancy entered the school.

The story of Saint Billiart is that despite her infirmity, she
spent hours in contemplation daily and received the sacra-
ments. During the French Revolution, she offered her home
as a refuge for priests and was hunted by authorities for the
sanctuary she offered. Ultimately, she received a vision one
day that directed her to develop an institute to serve young
women. When she was fifty-five years old, after five days of

prayer, she was somehow healed miraculously from her paralysis. She established the Sisters of Notre Dame and began establishing schools for young women throughout Europe and around the world. Her family's visits to the local church and the school made such an impression on Little Nancy that as a young girl she declared she wanted to be a priest. For a long time, no one had the heart to tell her that women were not allowed to be priests, but that spirit in her indicated a future in breaking barriers.

It was 1954 when she entered the school, the same year as the *Brown v. Board of Education* decision. Though Maryland did not secede from the Union during the Civil War, it still fell below the Mason-Dixon Line, making it a Southern state. It had been a slaveholding state, and the vestiges of slavery still ran deep.

When Nancy was growing up, all the signs of racism were evident around her; white and colored water fountains, segregated waiting rooms and lunch counters, and, sis, in 1955 one of the first sit-ins of the Civil Rights movement occurred only a few miles away from her home at Read's Drug Store. The store would allow African Americans to shop and purchase items, but they could not receive service at any of the lunch counters. In January, just a month after the Montgomery Bus Boycott began in Alabama, student activists from Morgan State College and the local Edmondson High staged a sit-in. Nancy was probably too young to participate in these events, but they undoubtedly were part of her awareness during her coming-of-age.

The Catholic Church had also begun to dramatically shift. When she was a child and during her parents' lifetime, Catholicism had been a mystical religion. The services were conducted in Latin, which most followers did not know. The priests turned their backs to the congregation while reading from the Bible. But many areas of the country and around the world were inventing new rules and practices. At the mass that Nancy attended, the priests started speaking in English and they started to face the congregation. Nancy famously said in an interview that when she began her rise within the Democratic Party, she was self-effacing with respect to her ambition: "I wasn't raised to run for office, I was raised to be holy." Decades later, when she was asked whether she hated President Trump, she clapped back with "I don't hate anyone. I was raised to have a heart full of love." Little Nancy could not train to be a priest while at Notre Dame, but with the moral imperative of the Civil Rights movement circling all around her, she could see a clear path for how to combine "holy" work with public service—two areas where even as a young girl Nancy felt most at home.

After high school, she set off on her own but took all that she learned with her. She left home on a Sunday while her dad was in the final months of his Senate campaign. She was the first in her family to get out of Baltimore for college, in

1958, enrolling at Trinity Washington University, an all-women school in Washington, DC. While in school she was a member of the Democratic Club and volunteered for the Kennedy for President Campaign in 1960. Nancy didn't know exactly what was ahead of her, but she was led by her heart and forged ahead.

THE HOMEMAKER

I'm a survivor, I'm not gon' give up.
I'm not gon' stop, I'm gon' work harder.
—Destiny's Child, "Survivor"

I t was the 1960s, the days when wearing a denim shirt and denim pants, with a brown leather satchel tugging at your chest all the way down to your hip, paired with thick round sunglasses could work, even in a pretty buttoned-up place like DC. It was the dawn of the women's liberation movement, and in 1961 Nancy was taking a class in African history at the prestigious Georgetown University, the oldest Catholic university in the United States, where she would meet her future husband, Paul Pelosi. *Yaasss.* But, sis, we can call him Perfect Paul. **wink**

She was still enrolled at Trinity three miles away but had come to Georgetown to take a class with the brilliant historian Carroll Quigley. Paul was attending Georgetown and working toward a bachelor of science degree in foreign service. He was extremely tall and had a gorgeous head of hair. He was twenty days younger than her, born on April 15, 1940, an Aries. Perfect Paul from San Fran had the intelligence to match his good looks and could spark and blaze Nancy's fire. And best of all, sis, he was as ambitious as a queen needs a man beside her to be. Sweet Pea could have had her pick of the litter at GW. She chose Paul. *Perfect!*

Nancy graduated from Trinity in 1962 with a bachelor of arts in political science and got a job as an intern receptionist for Daniel Brewster, who served as a senator from Maryland from 1963 to 1969. Brewster's politics were aligned with what was happening around Nancy. She'd participated in the Civil Rights rally at the Lincoln Memorial and was among the 250,000 demonstrators on the Mall, where Dr. Martin Luther King Jr. delivered his "I Have a Dream" speech.

Brewster voted in favor of the Civil Rights Act of 1964 (and 1968); the Voting Rights Act of 1965; and the confirmation of Thurgood Marshall to the Supreme Court in 1967. Nancy's duties under Brewster included handling administrative tasks like the mail or the phones, and planning events—all things Nancy was already well skilled in and happy to do. Politics in Washington is an art, and Nancy didn't know it yet, but she was a master in training since birth.

On September 7, 1963, Nancy married Perfect Paul at the Cathedral of Mary Our Queen (*wink*) in Baltimore, surrounded by family and friends who'd made the drive from Little Italy. Our young queen walked down the aisle in a white silk satin gown with a lacy train. The Pelosis moved to New York City, where Paul took a sexy job as a banker and earned a degree from the Stern School of Business at New York University, and also took a course at the Harvard Business School. Nancy didn't have any job prospects yet, so she followed him to the City of Dreams and started a family.

The lovebirds had kid after kid, to the sum of five. In approximately six years and one week, she had four daughters and one son (Oh. My. Gosh, Madam Speaker): Nancy "Corrine," Christine, Jacqueline, Paul Jr., and Alexandra. Mrs. Pelosi was her mother's daughter, and in *Madam Speaker*, longtime biographer Marc Sandalow described how she ran her home with precision. "As soon as the dinner table was cleared, it was set for breakfast. Each child was responsible for laying out their school uniform and shining their shoes, subject to mom's inspection. On weekdays there were ten slices of wheat bread laid out on the kitchen counter, with an assortment of lunch meats, condiments, five bags of pretzels and five apples. 'I'm not taking any complaints,' Pelosi would say, and, 'Let's have some cooperation.' On weekends, the five little Pelosis were dressed in matching outfits, which made it easier to spot them if one strayed away."

And that's how you run the world, girlz. *snap. snap.*

*   *   *

WHEN THE FAMILY moved to San Francisco in 1969, Paul made a small fortune as a financier and real-estate investor, while his wife concentrated on being a homemaker.

They lived in Presidio Terrace, a small, wealthy neighborhood. Paul was a native San Franciscan, so there was family and an established community there that Nancy could couch herself and the children in. But, like a queen, it was in the comfort of her own palace where she truly found her footing among the California tribe. Her brother in-law, Ronald, was well-known locally as a member of the board of supervisors. Since San Francisco is a consolidated city (the city is its own county), people elected to the county board of supervisors also take on the duties that a city councilmember would typically perform. Ronald was in the know; he had the contacts to introduce Nancy to the right people so she could put her skills to work as soon as she was able, which allowed her to become a power broker in politics long before she officially entered Congress. But initially she led from the outside, from the warmth of her cozy living quarters.

She began using her tony residence to organize charitable and Democratic Party fundraising receptions that were full of delicious food (in the way that an Italian woman knows how to put out a spread), fancy cocktails, and wall-to-wall political and business heavyweights. At these parties, Mrs. Pelosi played the classic role that women in power echelons have always played, like Pamela Harriman and Jacqueline Kennedy before her, using their social grace to create strategic relationships.

She had no plans of becoming a politician herself. Building these relationships and coalitions was not to serve or benefit her in any way. She was on a mission for the people, the causes, and the Democratic Party she believed in. The events she organized were those that she found to be most meaningful and exhilarating. She took pride in her political convictions, and the camaraderie found amid small talk, mozzarella sticks, and Manhattans could change the world. She was the perfect hostess for that cause.

As she managed the mechanics of party politics to advocate for candidates she supported, she met players on both ends of the Democratic spectrum and was able to gain the respect of them all. Still, she was looked at as the hostess—*read*: in her place, a woman who could throw a great party in support of the men who needed her. And everyone was comfortable with that. And she was good with that too . . . for the time being, anyway.

YEARS LATER PELOSI'S parties and her unwavering support as a political wingwoman would grow in influence and renown. Politics can be a tough environment to navigate. But even as a woman on the outside, she was influential. She was known for her cool, evenhanded way of dealing with the tension that inevitably surfaces when money, power, opportunity, and men collide. She knew how to handle the tight spaces in a patriarchal system; she had grown into girlhood in a house full of boys and had seen plenty of boys' clubs in action, so she would not be easily intimidated.

For decades before she came on the scene, San Francisco politics had two major factions: one headed by Leo McCarthy, a state assemblyman at the time Pelosi met him, and the other by Congressman Phil Burton. McCarthy represented the more business-minded, conservative Democratic camp, but Burton's camp had numbers on its side as the favorite among the street-savvy, unionized working class and the minorities in San Francisco.

Pelosi's tactical awareness made her able to gain respect in both camps, which takes us to a pivotal moment in her career that would shift the party's understanding of this homemaker's value, leading her to enter the stage, with hair blown back and Beyoncé glitter fluttering behind her.

So what had happened was:

Governor Jerry Brown was a latecomer to the presidential campaign of 1976. He had jumped in the race in an attempt to stop the momentum of a surging but relatively unknown candidate from Georgia named Jimmy Carter—he worried that Carter couldn't beat incumbent president Gerald Ford.

Brown decided it was time to offer the party another viable Democratic candidate. The problem was, the other candidates had been on the trail for a year or more—he was so late to the race that a few states had already held their primaries!

So Brown's campaign was a long shot, but when Pelosi heard that he was going to be campaigning on the East Coast, she wrote a memo to him suggesting that he concentrate more intently on Maryland. Brown had overlooked the Maryland primary because it carried only a small percentage of the delegates that would be required to win the Democratic nomination. Why go for a crumb when you can have the big piece of pie? is a common fallacy among politicians. But Pelosi knew better. Her father had taught her that the crumbs are what holds the pie together.

She convinced Brown that disregarding Maryland was a tactical error by reminding him that Maryland's primary took place just before California's. She recommended he view Maryland more dynamically, not simply in terms of its delegates but as an opening salvo to the California election. If he launched successfully in Maryland, it could turn the tide of his campaign in California and signal that he could win. She delivered that memo to Leo McCarthy, who shared it with Brown.

She recommended Brown get in touch with her brother Tommy III, who had by then served as president of the Baltimore City Council and mayor of the city. She also thought he should contact Ted Venetoulis, Baltimore's county executive—who had been her prom date in high school. (Yes, girlfriends, utilize your exes.) They had connections in the neighborhoods. When Brown was in Baltimore, he stayed at Pelosi's former home on Albemarle Street. Her brother and Venetoulis introduced him everywhere during his two-week visit, and in the end he won the Maryland primary.

Though Brown didn't become the nominee, his primary win in Maryland—and in California, right after—deepened his understanding of Pelosi's strategic value, and he and his buddies had an aha moment. He did not forget that it was Pelosi's shrewd, sound advice that had gotten him those wins. One Brown staffer called her "the secret weapon" of the Brown campaign, and she was rewarded. She was Brown's choice that year to represent California on the Democratic National Committee.

By then she was thirty-seven years old, and her children were safely tucked away at school during business hours. No one needed homework checked, and she could retire from being their personal chauffeur. Family still came first, but she finally had the time to really dig into the political scene and concentrate on her passion.

Suddenly, her two worlds—homemaker and political operative—merged even closer. Brown himself spent time sitting on her couch while she cooked meals for her family. Following her mother's example, she was in constant motion, making every minute count with persistent, determined effort, and penetrating the strategic heart of every issue. Sis, one California official caught a ride with her once and noticed that she had to gather up some handwritten notes on the front seat so he could sit down. It was clear she had been stuffing envelopes at stoplights during her short trip. Pelosi took her new role seriously (standard practice for an Aries queen). She knew all the players, and her disinterest in running for office herself allowed her to be an unvarnished ally to California politicians who needed help.

That's the focused energy of an up-and-coming *boss*.

★

BOSS LADY

Started from the bottom, now we're here.
Started from the bottom, now the whole team's here.
—Drake, "Started from the Bottom"

Within the dome of the Democratic National Committee, Nancy Pelosi could not dwell in her freshman role for long. The DNC is the overarching body for all the Democratic campaigns in the country that all our favorite politicians run under: for Alexandria Ocasio-Cortez, Auntie Maxine Waters, Elizabeth Warren, and all of the Queens of the Resistance, the DNC is the campaign arm. The organization offers assistance to candidates, including fundraising support and logistical resources, such as paid personnel and volunteers who fly in at critical moments during the campaign cycle. The DNC also looks out for key campaigns where more television ads, phone calls, polling data, and volunteers can make the most difference. Its largest role is fundraising, to ensure that the presidential nominee of the party, in particular, has the resources necessary to win the election. It's a winner's game. And Pelosi was a politically posh wunderkind and flourished as a fundraiser and Democratic aide. After Pelosi's first stint on the DNC, she served as chair of the Northern California Democratic Party from 1977 to 1981 and then chair of the California State Democratic Party from 1981 to 1983.

As chair, her mandate was simple: win elections. Pelosi had the stamina, the know-how, and the connections to do just that. When she first sat on the DNC, it required *millions of dollars* to win elections. Today it costs *hundreds of millions*. It all started with her calling on all those people she'd met at her parties over the years, a larger-scale version of what her father had done early in his career when he revisited the neighbors from his delivery route and insurance sales.

Her second plan of action was to streamline and upgrade party operations, develop the first permanent office for the party in Sacramento, computerize the data the party had gathered about voters, and commission the first statewide polls to gather more specific information on voter preferences. She founded the party's first headquarters at the Phelan Building on Market Street, where she worked while her children were at school. Her main daily tasks were to provide a means for expanding voter registration rolls and raising money or doing whatever it took to elevate the party.

She centralized her San Francisco office to include other

party officials whose offices had been scattered throughout the city. She gathered party operations in the city in one place so that people working for the same cause could know one another, communicate, negotiate, and collaborate, using her mother's strategy to centralize operations to make them more focused and empowered through personal connection.

She was willing to set high goals to achieve party aims. She challenged herself and her team to register a million new voters during her tenure, no matter what it took. And this was long before cell phones and the internet, sister. Those things were still just tools of the military. Initially, the party fell short of their overall goal, but with some Pelosi muscle they increased the rolls by 700,000 Democrats just as the Reagan revolution was about to take hold of Washington. Under Pelosi's leadership, California would become a Democratic stronghold, especially in its northern regions where her influence was greatest.

According to *Madam Speaker*, Nancy Pelosi once said about fundraising, "I hate it . . . I don't know anybody who enjoys it. I am good at it." Sandalow wrote, "Pelosi said her fundraising ability came from carefully listening to people and having a strong sense of what they were interested in. She was known for her incredible attention to detail, for sending donors gracious notes, their favorite flowers, or, in one case, a bottle of pomegranate bath oil to a supporter passionate about the fruit. She would set specific targets for potential donors and ask them only to contribute to candidates she felt were good matches."

In 1984, Pelosi used her clout and influence inside the DNC to bring the Democratic National Convention to San Francisco. Dianne Feinstein, then the mayor, was lukewarm to the idea. It required lots of fundraising, preparation for the influx of visitors, and the creation of a compelling program. Pelosi's style was always poised, consistent, slow to speak, and quick to listen. Confidently in control yet demanding in her expectations. If she wanted something, she'd get it. Command the facts, cover all the bases, keep the hair bob intact, and the need would take care of itself. Clearly Feinstein had underestimated this boss lady. So, Feinstein had to be convinced. Pelosi was smart enough to know that she couldn't go it alone. She brought with her men who represented the components necessary to win the day: Willie Brown, then head of the California State Assembly, and William Shorenstein, a big-money developer and friend of the party. Ultimately San Francisco won the bid, and that convention made history! Walter Mondale, the Democratic nominee, announced that Congresswoman Geraldine Ferraro would be his vice-presidential running mate. She was the first woman ever nominated by a major political party to serve as vice president.

Despite the fact that the convention ended on a high note, Mondale was trounced in the election, losing forty-nine of fifty states as Reagan sailed into a second term. In the wake of this devastating loss, Pelosi would endure one of the few defeats of her career. She had set her sights on becoming chair of the Democratic National Committee, and after engineering a successful convention, she should have had a great chance. Unfortunately, the party was licking its wounds after the Mondale–Ferraro defeat. Some of the stain of that debacle affected people's perceptions of Pelosi. They knew she could raise money like a pro. They knew she was poised and attractive. Some knew she had accomplished a great deal when she'd held state offices in California. Despite all of her achievements, those party leaders could not make the leap. They could not believe she would have the authority to negotiate with congressmen from East Coast and Southern states, who were much more conservative than they were in California.

So what did the boss lady do to convince these people that she could do the job?

She resisted their mind frame. She flew to Washington a week ahead of the vote to work rooms, meet delegates, and talk to reporters. She calmly underscored the fact that she had the credentials to lead.

But people still just didn't see a mother of five, a forty-two-year-old woman, as a power broker. Had she been a man, she would have eased into first position. Despite her best efforts, she realized that she could not win. She dropped out of the race a day before the vote. This strategy of folding when she knows she's beat would come to define her style as Speaker. She does not believe in failure, so she doesn't fail. She doesn't bring a bill to the floor that she is backing without being secure she has the votes for it to pass.

You think this is over-speak, eh? *Check it*, Pelosi grew up counting votes, so she is an expert, a high priestess, and has a discerning human nature for it. She can read you, read the votes, and read the members to determine whether they are sincere or just BSing her. These are the unspoken talents needed for politics. She will withhold a bill and continue to work to get the votes that are necessary, rather than bring a bill to the floor that is likely to fail. She's a queen and mother of five who can predict with accuracy how it will go.

In the case of her run for DNC chair, her flawless, meticulous approach to every issue may have been detrimental to her this one time. She was so good at what she did as a state party chair, people could not imagine her doing anything else. Her talents for getting things done were perhaps too subtle. If she had to become firm, she'd do it behind closed doors. She's not the loudmouth at the supermarket calling out the cashier about the long lines. She's smooth and has a plan. Her defeat was only temporary. She would learn from her mistakes and subtly shift her game.

She would not stop.

AFTER THE DNC chair debacle, Pelosi was called to serve as the finance chair of the Democratic Senate Campaign Committee, or DSCC. The DSCC is an organization similar to the DNC, but its focus is only on US Senate elections to ensure that the special needs of a Senate race are assisted strategically and financially by the party. Only a third of the one hundred senators run at a time. And as DSCC finance chair, Pelosi had the chance to really shine. As usual, she helped make a dramatic difference.

In this role her strategy and diplomacy only got bigger, and she was delivering on a grand scale, honey. She traveled around the country hosting events, including a big fundraiser at the home of Barbra Streisand (*ahhhhh!!!!*). The longtime Democratic supporter performed fourteen songs for invited guests, hoping to whet their appetite for generosity. It was seduction like no other. As usual, Pelosi was on the winning side. Reagan's popularity was down due to the Iran–Contra scandal, and the president had become more reclusive after a near miss with death when he was shot by a deranged man.

In that loco climate, Democrats regained majority control of the Senate by winning eight seats.

Pelosi was again a champion, but she had won more than just a series of elections. She won powerful allies in the elected senators and cred in the streets. Senators who were once busy were now often willing to answer her calls. *Truth, sis:* members of Congress are more concerned about their constituents than any other voices. So unless you got pull with those people, for the most part you should expect to be sent to voicemail. And outside heat from members who may or may not understand their concerns often goes ignored, but not in Pelosi's case. No way, José. Pelosi had raised the money that helped them win. These loyalties would come in handy when Pelosi would become a member of Congress herself.

Pelosi was smart: she kept her cards close to the vest. She was "operational," as one politician called her, meaning her focus was always on getting things done, and she was trust-worthy. All the boys on the Hill understood that her "yes" meant "yes" and her "no" meant "no." She was never caught up in the vanities of politics that led other prima donnas to boast or seek attention. She commanded the room due to her power in getting results. She also allowed those working with her to shine too. She was the kind of leader who made the major and minor players equals.

This delicate, detailed approach to relationships within the party makes her one of the most effective fundraisers on the Democratic side, and it is one reason she is able to win reelection to office repeatedly. Many career politicians, especially in the House, have such skills. But it takes a mighty woman to win elections for more than three decades.

Pelosi was doing her job well, but unfortunately there was a lot going on in the political landscape that would force her to work even harder.

★

MOTHER IN CHIEF

B y the mid-1980s, Pelosi's daughter Alexandra was still
at home, but finishing up high school. All the other
children had already sailed toward adulthood and independence. And Pelosi had even more expressly made their
San Francisco home a hub for political salons where Democrats could have an open mic to speak (*oh, how these politicians like to talk and talk and talk*) with constituents about
issues ranging from environmentalism to economics.

But it was a woman, Sala Burton, with her brains and swag,
who could see more in Nancy Pelosi. Sala was a Polish American congresswoman in the San Francisco Bay Area. She was
born in Białystok, Poland. In 1939, when she was fourteen
years old, she fled Poland along with her parents to escape the
Nazi invasion and occupation. Sala framed her passion for politics in these words, which should inspire any queen reading

this who has thought about getting involved in politics: "I saw and felt what happened in Western Europe when the Nazis were moving. You learn that politics is everybody's business. The air you breathe is political—it isn't just a game for certain people. We must all be vigilant in terms of whom we elect to office, vigilant in terms of our civil rights and liberties."

On her deathbed, she proposed an idea that would upset a lot of people, but she had a nation to think about, not the feelings of the boys in Congress. Her idea was to designate Nancy Pelosi the holder of her seat until there could be a special election. She knew Nancy could jump in and handle it. They were women with that in common. A queen knows a queen.

Sala had been up against a similar obstacle when her husband, Phil Burton, died. (Remember Phil? He repped the San Fran working class when Pelosi was new on the scene.) Sala and Phil had met at the California Democratic Convention in the 1950s, and after decades of marriage and life together in Washington, DC, Phil died while still serving a term in 1983. Within eight days, Sala had to step up to take his unexpired seat temporarily. She decided to run for the seat in the special election that then took place. There were men foaming at the mouth for that seat, but she had to be courageous. After her own career in Democratic politics, she had the right skills and attitude: "I'm not running because I'm a woman. I'm running because I think I can do more in Congress than anyone." She was successful, and held the seat for two terms, but during a third election, she was diagnosed with colon cancer. She won the race but was unable to leave the hospital to take the oath of office.

In her final days, she called her dear friend Nancy. The woman who had tirelessly worked alongside her father, a woman who had grown up in Little Italy and understood the struggles of immigrants. Sala wanted someone who could "represent the dispossessed, the hungry, the poor, the children, people in trust territories, the aged—those people who don't have a lot of lobbying being done for them." She saw Nancy's value, and even though there were a bunch of others who probably had more experience, maybe even more knowledge of the job, she knew Nancy had what was most important: the good heart and will. If she was going to leave behind the work that she and her husband had done, she would leave it with Nancy Pelosi. Men were banging down the door for her seat, and, again, she would make a decision that would piss a lot of people off.

The boys cried, oh did the boys cry, and complain. And of course some women did too. What had Sala Burton done by giving her seat to some homemaker? They were just haters. But what did Nancy think? Nancy didn't want it either . . . Well, she had to think about it.

Again, she had not ever thought of herself in Congress. She was used to being in the background like she had been her whole life, by her dad's side or behind her husband . . . but never in front. The DNC chair seat was close enough. She had made an impact there. She didn't need to be center stage, right? She had children. Though they were older now, she was still worried about abandoning her family. Finally, she asked her daughter's advice:

> I went to her and said: "Alexandra, Mommy has a chance to run for Congress. I don't know if I'll win but I want to know what you think. I can stay here with you because you have one more year at home or I could run for Congress."
>
> To which she said, "Mother," and I knew I was in trouble right there and then, "Mother, get a life." And so I got another life and went off to Congress. And she then said, "Mother, what teenager doesn't want her mother gone three nights a week?"

Yes, it would require a lot, and Nancy knew just exactly how much from working with her dad. But she'd been a mom—the most important assignment in the world—and raised five little humans. She had sewn Halloween costumes (even angels with silver wings!), carpooled, chaperoned field trips, made chocolate cupcakes, and faced her children's every need and challenge with them, as the fixer, the hugger, the healer, and the referee in enough sibling rivalries to qualify for the WWE. It would be a three-thousand-mile commute away from her husband and kids. But if motherhood didn't teach her anything else, it taught her that she was powerful. If there was such a force as a superwoman, then it was she, along with the rest of the moms she knew. Nancy said: Yes! Yes! Yes!!! to the job.

This would be her first run for Congress. Her first time on the other side of the microphone. Though her career in modernizing the Democratic Party and helping to get others elected had been characterized by success after success, somehow the men in charge were consistent in looking past everything she had accomplished. Just like they did in her run for DNC chair, they just *still* could not or would not see her in a leadership position.

Sis, the election took place during a difficult time for the community in San Francisco. Less than a decade had passed since the 1978 assassinations of Harvey Milk, the first openly gay person elected to San Francisco's Board of Supervisors, and Mayor George Moscone. The tragedy was one of the worst in the city's history, and sadness hung heavy in people's hearts. The gay community was devastated by the loss of Milk. He had pioneered activism that freed them from a life in the shadows. Added to this, people were dying every day in San Francisco due to AIDS, and President Reagan refused to acknowledge the crisis or even mention the disease. San Franciscans needed someone to go to Washington who could make sure the federal government understood the pressing needs of the city and the nation.

Pelosi's campaign decided her greatest advantage in the race was that she could get things done in Washington through her connections. Her slogan was "Nancy Pelosi: A Voice That Can Be HEARD!" There was a learning curve, to be sure, but ultimately she prevailed against fourteen candidates to win the special election to succeed Sala Burton.

She received a bedside endorsement from Rep. Burton a month before she was sworn in and a week before the revered congresswoman passed away.

The impact of Burton's choice to support Pelosi's run for Congress would ultimately heighten respect for female leadership in this country, and it would send one of the nation's top strategists to Washington during an era that would bring attacks on all the progressive advances made during Phil and Sala Burton's lives. Nancy Pelosi would promote the causes of women's rights, gay rights, and voting rights, but during a hostile, bitter time in politics.

She would come to lead the charge clothed in her Armani suits and Chanel sunglasses, but her image would be constantly distorted by the men who hate and want to trade in visceral, sexist stereotypes to win elections. They would try as hard as they could to destroy her upper hand, but she would prevail against the best, against all the unending attacks they could send her way. And she would go on to serve in Congress for more than thirty years, oversee the largest women's caucus of House members in American history, and become an icon whose life is a master class in leadership, like a *boss*.

★ ★ ★ ★ ★ ★ ★ ★ ★ ★ ★ ★ ★

LEADER

Power is not
anything that's given
away. Power is
something you have
to compete for.

—NANCY PELOSI, INTERVIEW WITH
HARPER'S BAZAAR, JULY 16, 2008

⭐

MI CHIAMO
CONGRESSWOMAN PELOSI

I learned to love myself unconditionally
Because I am a queen.
—India.Arie, "Video"

The first thing Nancy did as Congresswoman Pelosi was quit cooking. That's it (*cue hands slapping*), done. It took her a minute to catch on to this new reality, but her new life by design no longer required kitchen duty. "I always had the salad and set the table, but I didn't have to clean the pots." There was neither remorse nor guilt. She had been loyal and raised healthy children. *Cooking, this relationship is over! Queen exits.* "My daughter Alexandra once told me, 'Mother, you're a pioneer. Now hardly anybody cooks, but you were one of the first to stop.' After twenty years of cooking, I started to appreciate the value of other people's work. So I would, say, go get a duck in Chinatown."

It was a good thing too—she had a lot of work ahead of her. Since her first win in 1987, Congresswoman Pelosi won reelection on the reg, dominating like a queen every time with as much as (and often more than) 80 percent of the vote.

As soon as she took office, her life became a new kind of balancing act. Nancy Pelosi is a decision-maker, but she's also infused with energy and creativity. She calls it like it is but maintains an air of warmth and playfulness. She can do one-on-one girlfriend chatter about chocolate and the importance of self-care and bubble baths at the end of a hard day's work. This is how she's survived the concrete jungle of Capitol Hill into her eighties and how she's still going without slowing down. In fact, she takes a bubble bath each day, with a dish of dark chocolate and a crossword puzzle or book by her side (which could range from Gabriel García Márquez to Doris Kearns Goodwin). She knows how to stop and smell the roses after an all-nighter in the field with the big bad wolves—that's how she stays so *fly*.

That's Pelosi. She's a master at diplomacy. She's a force with numbers. So much so that she knows exactly how many times to wash her face to maintain her good looks. (Thirty splashes, exact. No less. She says, "If it's twenty-five, oh my gosh, I'm going to fall apart.") She's grace and elegance, a badass and control all rolled into one woman. And she's no animal about challenges. No biggie. More chocolate, please.

So, in 1987, when the new congresswoman arrived fresh on Capitol Hill, she was no Dorothy in the land of Oz: thankfully, because of her father's time there, she knew it well. But still, it was exciting. Landing in DC with her two stilettos firmly planted on the ground as an elected official felt glorious! Capitol Hill is not a place adorned with flowers. It is grand and intimidating and can be a little dark once you're on the inside. Six white marble buildings seal in the city—structures that are so enormous in size and scope, they quickly humble even the biggest of giants. It houses more than ten thousand workers, tunnels, subways, and its own federal police force. The Capitol Building is ornate and impressive, filled with symbols of the country's founding—sculptures, paintings, gold leaf on some of the rotunda ceilings, imposing statues, and an overpowering history of America's legacy. It is where presidents make their State of the Union addresses and, within its chambers, where lawmakers of the House and Senate cast their votes on change-making policies. All of it would become Nancy's home sweet home for the next few decades.

She walked the halls seeking her office, which was small. Maybe a closet, but okay. Members' offices are on either side of the Capitol; there are three House buildings and three Senate buildings. The Speaker has a series of suites in the Capitol, as do the majority and minority leadership: the majority and minority party leaders, the majority and minority whips, and powerful committee chairs. Every time the House changes hands, meaning when Republicans or Democrats lose control of the majority, all of these offices are shifted like a rotation of musical chairs, so that whichever party is in the majority gets to preside in the Capitol offices. The opposition party members are left on their butts and must scavenge like hyenas for office shelter. Minority leaders have offices in the Capitol also, but they are harder to find, much smaller, and less ornate.

It's a place full of overachievers, A+ students, graduates with honors, valedictorians, Ivy Leaguers, you know, private school kids, scholarship and merit winners—hence the constant pee-in-your-pants paranoia! It is also a place where anyone able to win an election—definitely a formidable task—can take a seat. Members of the House can be schoolteachers, the Mothers of the Movement (hello, Congresswoman Lucy McBath), airline hostesses, bartenders (hello, AOC), labor leaders, nurses (hello, Lauren Underwood), police officers, ministers. That's the growing rough-and-tumble beauty of the House today: all kinds are being represented.

So, in June 1987, when Speaker of the House Jim Wright swore in Nancy Pelosi, a fortysomething woman, with the oath of office, it was a special day. Her entire family was there, with both Big Tommy and Big Nancy beside her. Though new members are allotted very little speaking time on the floor, due to their lack of seniority, Pelosi had wondered if she would have an opportunity to say anything at all at her swearing in. She was told she would not, but much to her surprise, an officer of the House, likely at Wright's direction, asked whether she might want to say a few words. So she did, speaking off the cuff in her typical composed and elegant style. She mentioned the plights of the Burtons, for whom she mourned, and wished for their presence. She also went for it and made a statement that would let the nation know she was not there to kid around. Her first words to her colleagues as an elected official were "My name is Nancy Pelosi and I'm here to fight AIDS."

It was bold and gutsy. *Boom*, the queen had arrived.

After being sworn in, she had to find her place on a committee. Her father had been a member of the Appropriations Committee. As he was wheeled past Speaker Wright on the day of her swearing in, he angled for her appointment there as well. The Appropriations Committee is very powerful because its members have the ability to regulate, fight for, and oversee how trillions of dollars in government funding will be allocated to the federal agencies. They can ensure that funding is directed toward needs that are vital to their districts and debate the priorities and methods to use to distribute federal dollars. Such an important committee assignment is usually not granted to a freshman member, but Pelosi would find herself there soon enough.

Members do have an opportunity to indicate which committee assignments they would prefer, and Speaker Wright offered Pelosi two advantageous placements. She joined the House Committee on Government Operations, which has

since been restructured and renamed the House Committee on Government Oversight and Reform. The committee's function was to oversee the economy, efficiency, management, and functioning of all the federal agencies. Today the committee also oversees the management of the post office and the city of Washington, DC, itself.

Sis, Nancy had done her homework, as usual. Her research revealed that a position on this committee, though not considered a plum post at the time, would give her a strategic vantage point to encourage the Food and Drug Administration to make approvals for experimental AIDS treatments a higher priority. She was also placed on the Banking, Finance, and Urban Affairs Committee, which has also since been restructured and renamed. It is now called the House Committee on Financial Services, headed by another Queen of the Resistance today, Rep. Maxine Waters. This committee regulates the entire financial services industry, including securities, insurance, banking, and housing. It also oversees the Federal Reserve, the Treasury Department, and the Securities and Exchange Commission.

Pelosi saw the committee's jurisdiction of housing finance as a means to help devise strategies to offer dying members of the gay community much-needed housing—many of them were rendered homeless by landlords who feared renting to people who had the disease.

What Nancy lacked in experience she made up for in confidence. Even newly landed in DC, she knew how to operate to make things happen. She also knew that she would have an uphill battle on her hands. When Pelosi stepped into the chamber, the 100th Congress had twenty-four women, half of them Democrats and half of them Republicans. According to *Madam Speaker*, "At that time there no women pages, no women on the Capitol police force, and virtually no women reporters."

But she was not intimidated by being the sole woman anywhere, honey.

Besides, Nancy Pelosi had a decided advantage, one that would be noted and mindfully replicated as closely as possible by other members seeking to climb the ranks of the House. Despite the fact that she had not begun her career with a tour of duty on Capitol Hill as her goal, Pelosi could never have been better positioned. Because she had aided in the campaigns of so many Democratic representatives around the country, she already knew nearly half of the 435 members of Congress by name. As campaign finance became even more important to electoral success, Pelosi's ability to raise money, to leverage her incredible network of influential friends to contribute to candidates' campaigns, and to capitalize on her ingenuity and influence as a legislator made her a force to be reckoned with, even at the beginning of her tenure. She was in her element and loving it even more than she imagined.

For a freshman member, advantages are few. The House, in particular, is an institution where the most senior members have the most power. Everything is awarded by seniority, from the selection of office spaces to committee placements, and even the speaking order at news conferences. Longevity is the key to the kingdom, which is why retaining long-serving members is beneficial to constituents. They have the power to take the lead on issues important to voters. New members, mainly, do not. A new member's goal is to develop more strategic ways to affect outcomes, since traditional power is not on their side. This dynamic played to freshman congresswoman Pelosi's strengths and helped to distinguish her ability to make good on her promises.

In true Pelosi fashion, she wasted no time jumping into the hectic life on the Hill. Days for House members are incredibly busy: long meetings with constituents and other politicians, demanding hearings, spur-of-the-moment press conferences, and votes during the day; and fundraisers, caucus gatherings, galas, and keynote speeches at night. It is a 24/7, nonstop cycle of activity and hustle. And let's get one thing straight right now—recess does *not* mean members and their staffs aren't working. Recess simply means there are no scheduled votes on the floor of the House. When the House is not in session or is on recess for several days, like during the weekend, members return home to their districts and work out of their district offices. There, members take meetings with business leaders, city and state legislators, and everyday people they represent who are having problems. They are often as busy in the district offices as they are in Washington. Got it? Recess equals no votes but still includes nonstop work. If the new congresswoman had known hard work before, she was now entering the beast arena, Ninja Warrior zone.

But, sis, she would *slaayy*!

When members are back from recess, all votes must take place in person in Washington. Votes are called by the leader of the party that controls the majority. They are not scheduled long in advance, so Pelosi would have to learn to bring her A game on the fly. Members must cast their votes themselves, with few exceptions, within the recorded period allotted, generally fifteen minutes. Thus they spend very little time away from the Capitol campus unless they are assured votes will not be called for several hours.

House members outside of the leadership do not have much say in when a vote is called, but a lot can be done to "hotline," or fuel passage of, a bill. A successful politician is a strategist who has the influence, the contacts, and the knowledge to get legislation passed.

Nancy Pelosi's rise into the House demonstrates that experience in politics is critical to getting things done in Washington. She had been born into it. She maintained the persuasive voice that had helped her navigate spaces like this for decades: firm but careful. She was more interested in action than anything else, and laser-focused on her agenda. If she ever suffered indignity at the hands of some bawdy, entitled male members of Congress, she never discussed it publicly. She once said, "As long as they can't take my children from me, I'm not afraid of anything."

PELOSI IS A fierce competitor who de-escalates each challenge presented, and she can make her preferences stick. But if Pelosi's life and responsibilities went into overdrive with her move to Congress, she had the chops to move with them. Her goal was never to be perfect but always to get the job done. According to Sandalow in *Madam Speaker*, "As a working woman, Pelosi could be quite scattered. She constantly left her purse behind, lost her wallet, and regularly misplaced envelopes of cash that her staff had prepared for her. She brought piles of constituent mail on airplanes, rarely allowing herself enough time to get through the stack, and would end up lugging it back and forth, trip after trip. She lost expensive jewelry, including a Bulgari necklace, on her cross-country flights."

But Nancy exhibited no signs of imposter syndrome. She was described as "intensely focused."

All this to say, she was human like the rest of us, yet a class act of her own.

In her first week, she appointed someone who could help advance her AIDS agenda. Her goal was to get legislation passed as soon as possible to assist the AIDS-affected communities of her district. Everybody told her that as a freshman member, it would probably be impossible. Still, her top priority was to demonstrate to members that AIDS was an epidemic that presented a public health threat, not just to the gay community but to all of the American communities.

She worked with her staff and the legislative counsel to write AIDS-related bills within her first two months of office. Then Claude Pepper, the chairman of the powerful Rules Committee, which governs the conditions and rules by which a bill comes to the floor of the House, allowed her bills to move forward.

She also set about getting as much buy-in to her bills as possible from members on both sides of the aisle in those early days. She made sure her staff wrote releases that never took full credit for the work, and was willing at press conferences to share the limelight with other members.

Coalition building was the key to passage, so she set about persistent work to build relationships with fellow members who could support the action. This age-old process is the cornerstone of the political arena.

The goal is to enfranchise as many co-signers to the legislation as possible to help persuade those who might still remain on the sidelines, if the bill comes up to a vote. Then comes the process of whipping.

Whipping, as it's called in political terminology, is a persuasive process that brings all of leadership's knowledge of an individual member of Congress to bear to encourage them to vote with leadership. What are the major concerns of their district, what bills are they trying to get passed, where does their wife work, where do their children go to school, who is their hometown pastor, which House members are their drinking buddies, and which are their adversaries? All of these questions, and many more, have answers, which are used by a "whip organization" to persuade a member to cast a vote for a leadership-backed bill.

Pelosi, though a novice and a woman, had made enough inroads with other members that she had some whipping power, and they were willing to sit down with her. She had done the research, so she knew which places in the country, and thus which congressional districts, were most deeply affected by or vulnerable to the AIDS crisis. She also brought the facts to members who might be on the fence about whether there was an epidemic or not. This is the heart of the political process, and it is this kind of influence that voters need to consider as we go to the polls. Who among the candidates has the best ability to tactically and capably deliver on legislative ideas that represent our values? Everyone likes a charming candidate, but it's about who can deliver! Sis, you don't want to back a pretty face and find your needs not met.

Pelosi never took a win for granted, but she also felt that

losing was not an option when so many lives were at stake. She continued her advocacy relentlessly, inviting members to field hearings in her San Francisco district so they could hear the stories of survivors themselves. Many times, these efforts happen behind the scenes, where reporters are not able to enter. Legislative proposals like Pelosi's can get subsumed under larger bill packages for a variety of reasons that reporters never see.

When Pelosi would go home to San Francisco, she would hear stories of men dying in ratty, low-rent hotels because their employers feared their illness, which cost them their jobs and homes. Pelosi's goal was to get aid to those infected with the virus by getting health benefits in alignment with their needs. The COBRA law provided up to eighteen months of group health coverage in cases like this, but it would take twenty-nine months before they would be eligible for Medicare coverage, which caused them to be solely responsible out of pocket for eleven months of medical coverage. These sorts of loopholes were devastating to families. Pelosi set her sights on getting AIDS patients (as well as other people with disabilities) group insurance until Medicare coverage was available. She also worked to get those with Social Security to qualify for disability payments and for all the patients to be eligible to receive home care.

As a lawmaker, to help resolve the problem, Pelosi co-wrote a bill that would offer federal subsidies to housing organizations and businesses that would allow AIDS patients to live there. She wrote bills that provided a way for large cities with affected populations, like Los Angeles, San Francisco, and New York, to share data. She mailed a copy of the surgeon general's thirty-six-page report, which offered guidance on safe practices, to every home in her district. The report also offered information to dispel myths about how the disease was spread. Many people didn't know AIDS could not be contracted by shaking hands, coming into contact with the tears of the affected, coughing, or sneezing.

She formed alliances with fellow legislators as well as activists like Cleve Jones, founder of the NAMES Project. She helped to negotiate with the National Park Service to bring the AIDS Memorial Quilt to the National Mall. The quilt contains original artwork with thousands of panels honoring the lives of those lost in the AIDS epidemic. Pelosi was among those who read the 1,920 names on the quilt as people wept. The AIDS quilt eventually grew to 40,000 panels.

When the administration of President H. W. Bush did not want to seem to contradict Reagan's denial of the epidemic or alienate the support of the Moral Majority, a religious right-wing coalition, by singling out the disease as a target for federal funds through specific legislative action, Pelosi compromised by allowing the federal government to distribute nonspecific state funding so they could give it to communities most affected by the disease.

She also, in 1990, coauthored the Ryan White Act, named after a young hemophiliac boy in Indiana who was not allowed to attend school after contracting AIDS from a blood transfusion. School officials acted out of a baseless fear that he posed a risk to the health of other students. He died in 1990. The Ryan White bill first allocated $220 million to the hardest-hit cities. Today it has been responsible for tens of billions of dollars of federal support to combat the disease. When Republicans took control of Congress in 1994, they worked to strip almost $40 million in support from AIDS-related bills, including the Ryan White Act. Pelosi, then a member of the Appropriations Committee, fought back. She used her power on the committee to restore the funding. Hurrah!

AS A FRESHMAN member Pelosi worked at top speed. She went into the job with an agenda and pulled out all the weeds to get down to the root of where she could best serve the country. There weren't enough hours in a day to accomplish all that she wanted, but it would be a fight every day, and she'd meet each challenge on its own terms.

Her life had changed swiftly. She was traveling back and forth between Washington and San Francisco, an almost six-hour trip, about forty times a year. She traveled roughly eight hundred round trips or 4 million miles, the equivalent of 160 tours around the world. Even for someone like Pelosi, who'd had an intricate, detailed immersion into the world of politics from youth, it's not easy. It's a constant walk in the hard direction on the Hill. Pelosi was grindin', and she made things happen. But there was always work to do. She's the sort of woman who makes it look easy, but it isn't. Especially not all the time. Though Pelosi was a freshman on campus, she was also a woman of a certain age, playing on a court with people both much older and younger coming to her for help as the representative of the district. Pelosi is celebrated for her strength, but her best attribute continues to be her willingness to play along for our benefit. She could have retired nicely in the nest of her home. But she has always reached into those dark corners of the world where suffering is an open wound, and as a Queen of the Resistance, she is courageous in her endeavor to pull in light and hope, and set America back on a moral course. And in turbulent times, that's just comforting.

---★---

CAPTAIN OF THE RESISTANCE

I came to win, to fight, to conquer, to thrive
I came to win, to survive, to prosper, to rise.
—Nicki Minaj, feat. Rihanna, "Fly"

During Pelosi's first campaign in 1987, one member of San Francisco's Board of Supervisors questioned her ability to comprehend the struggles of most people's day-to-day life. She had never had to worry about childcare, to meet a payroll, to raise her children alone, to send her children to public school. Pelosi responded, "I don't think you have to be sick to be a doctor, or poor to understand the problems of the poor."

But if there were any doubt that she served her constituencies or that she was prepared to deliver on national or international issues that concerned them, her representation of Chinese constituents during the Tiananmen Square incident sealed the deal.

In 1989, pro-democracy Chinese students overtook Beijing's Tiananmen Square. They staged a massive sit-in lasting from April 15 until June 4, when the Chinese government declared martial law and used military force to disperse the protest. A huge battalion of as many as 250,000 troops entered the square during the night and opened fire on the protesters. By government estimates as many as 2,700 people were killed and 10,000 arrested. The violence of the military intervention shocked the world, and world leaders condemned the bloody manner in which the Chinese government intervened against the protests of its own citizens. The US Congress imposed economic sanctions against China in response to the vicious outcome of the military action.

Pelosi, as a representative for one of the largest populations of Chinese residents outside of mainland China, knew she had to do something. She quickly introduced legislation that would protect the 40,000 Chinese students studying in America whose visas required them to return home as soon as their studies were completed. Pelosi's bill sought to waive those requirements so that those students in her district and others around the United States would not be compelled to return to danger in their home country.

President George H. W. Bush offered to waive the visa requirement for a year. Pelosi was adamant that a year was not long enough. Sis, her bill offered students a four-year waiver and set ground rules that would enable them to stay in the States permanently. By midsummer, she had gathered 258 cosponsors for her bill. It passed through the Judiciary Committee without any resistance and was unanimously passed by the House.

The president was concerned about the measure, as he worried that the Chinese government might retaliate by ending student exchanges altogether if they could come to the United States as students and become permanent residents. He threatened to veto the bill, and in response, students rallied in support of the thousands of Chinese students who had been arrested, tortured, and even killed by their own government. Pelosi made it plain in her commentary during the media coverage of the US student protests that the president was the only encumbrance to the bill. She wanted to send a message from the government of the United States that "as long as [the Chinese government] continues to massacre its young people, the United States will not send them back." And she warned the president that if he vetoed the bill, Congress would move to override his veto.

Bush made good on his promise and vetoed the bill. Pelosi took up the challenge, applying the same relentless organizing ability that she used in the campaign to advocate on behalf of her legislation. It did not matter that she had only been a member of Congress for two years, and that Bush not only had been vice president under Reagan but had held public office and high posts in the Republican Party for years. She stayed on the House floor constantly lobbying both Democratic and Republican members. She called as many as thirty House members a day. She held a news conference on the steps of the Capitol with Chinese students. She even made sure she was invited to testify at a Senate hearing on the matter.

After more than a month of this tough political action, the House voted to override the veto by a vote of 390 for and 25 against. Her legislation had won in the House, but the Senate override effort was even tougher. It takes 67 votes to override a president's veto in the Senate. The Senate majority leader could only muster 62.

The bill had ultimately failed, but not without a tremendous show of strength by Madam Pelosi. It was nearly unheard-of for a woman and a freshman member to be so aggressive in her convictions. She made it plain that she was a powerhouse behind the scenes who knew how to use the advantages she had been given and that she had positioned herself to make the wheels of Congress turn to her rhythm and use them to serve the will of the people. And people in the House betta *recognize*.

PELOSI'S EFFORTS TO protect her constituents and stand up to Chinese government abuses then took another turn—trade. She began to advocate for tying US trade with China to progress on human rights inside the nation.

Knowing that the most stringent restrictions could not be

signed into law due to trade proponents in the Senate, Pelosi crafted a more strategic bill that would permit trade, as long as China released its political prisoners and made significant steps toward human-rights changes. Pelosi had read the tea leaves, and though she may have preferred more punitive measures, she realized some deterrent was better than no deterrent at all. This is politics, to find vehicles that build toward a vision of the future that can be realized.

Those who think compromise is a dirty word probably haven't spent any time trying to get things done in government; to take action without compromise would require replacing negotiation with force. The ideal goal in the political arena is the ability to work toward a solution mandated or inspired by the will of the people, and to navigate all the forces within the House, the Senate, and the White House to get there. To make things even more complicated, the House changes its composition every two years, the Senate changes in a rolling six years, and the White House can change every four years. Control of the House and Senate can also potentially change, so the variables that can affect the passage of a bill change constantly as well.

A shrewd politician always operates in favor of their party but retains relationships on both sides of the aisle so that their legislation has a chance at passage, regardless of who controls Congress or the White House. Pelosi herself once voiced her distaste for candidates who "speak of the word compromise as unprincipled—when it is, indeed, an art. If you compromise your principles, that is not a good thing."

Pelosi came to the Hill with these capabilities already in place. The only assets she didn't have yet were seniority and a position of leadership. But for the time being, her compromise bill had the right ingredients. It passed both the House and the Senate, but President Bush vetoed it again. It was stacking up to be a battle of wills between the White House and this talented freshman congresswoman.

Instead of backing down, Pelosi drove straight into the center of the conflict. She decided to lead a congressional delegation to China to meet with political leaders. While there, she was hoping to meet with political dissidents still imprisoned since the Tiananmen Square incident. Officials in Beijing denied her access. At a news conference in China, she talked about the possibility of revoking China's trade status and the release of political activists. During her trip, the delegation was received warmly by officials in Beijing, but Pelosi was not sidetracked. Between a ceremonious visit to the Great Wall and a scheduled dinner with the Chinese foreign minister, Pelosi and the two congressional members who had accompanied her on the trip snuck out of the hotel and headed to Tiananmen Square. In front of the Monument to the People's Heroes, they held white cloth roses and read a statement as crowds and news cameras gathered. They placed their flowers on the pavement and unrolled a banner they had smuggled into the country. It read, TO THOSE WHO DIED FOR DEMOCRACY IN CHINA, in both Chinese and English.

They were immediately confronted by Chinese guards, who began to jostle reporters. A skirmish occurred. Pelosi and her colleagues were able to cross the square, hop in a car, and get away. Several journalists from American news agencies were arrested and held by the police but eventually let go. Pelosi was reported to have been remarkably calm throughout the conflict, "almost regal," said one member who accompanied her. Pelosi said the police had overreacted and that their response contradicted assertions they were given during their trip that free speech was protected by the Chinese government.

When she visited China two years later as a member of the House Intelligence Committee, she did not back down when asked to evaluate her actions in retrospect. She never apologized, and she considers it to this day one of the proudest moments of her career.

THE POWER OF THE PURSE

This is America. . . .
We just wanna party.
—Childish Gambino, "This Is America"

The House of Representatives holds the purse strings of Congress. The Senate has some financial duties, but the House, baby, is the only agency of the government that can tax and spend public money. And our lady knows how to handle a purse, honey. *snap. snap.*

The United States is a representative democracy, which means that not every single eligible voter votes on every single issue of government. Instead we elect feisty badasses like Nancy Pelosi to vote and make decisions on our behalf. And all the children know that when Mother makes a decision, it's law. That's why the House of Representatives is considered the People's House, because *we* have always decided who goes in those seats. Senators were actually appointed by a governor or elected by a legislature until 1913, when the Seventeenth Amendment was enacted and we started electing senators by popular vote. The Senate was constructed by the founding fathers to ensure the minority opinions held by the more privileged, educated classes would not be simply overwhelmed by popular opinion. So, Pelosi and the other House members have their eyes focused on the regular ol' folks like you and me, sis.

During Pelosi's third year in Congress, she was able to follow her father's advice, using her connections and respect built through her strong leadership on the China issue, in particular, to secure a seat on the powerful Appropriations Committee.

The Appropriations Committee is überpowerful because it is responsible for how the government allocates all its discretionary funds. Think of it like this: there are two pots of cash in the federal budget. One is mandatory spending and the other is discretionary spending, which means the appropriators, also known as cardinals, have the power to decide how the government will spend all of its discretionary dollars.

Prior to the Civil War, when some financial shenanigans occurred, there was mainly just one financial committee of Congress, the House Ways and Means Committee, which made decisions about how federal dollars should be spent, allocated to the big banks, and regulated the expenditure of those funds. But, ugh, after some of the boys engaged in some dubious activities with the money, the jurisdiction divided the group up into multiple committees.

Here's what our lady found herself privy to on the Appropriations Committee. First, a budget resolution is created by the Budget Committee and voted on. The president's budget is his wish list. He can wish for a unicorn and even if one exists it's not going to happen unless it's been voted in by the committee. The president does not hold the purse strings. The House can use the president's budget as a guideline or not. He can stop payments allocated by Congress but does not have the power to decide how federal discretionary money can be spent. He does have executive authority to take certain steps in an emergency, and it seems like there have been a lot of emergencies declared in recent years. Mm-hmm, *side-eye*. He also has his own discretionary budget that he can spend as he chooses, within guidelines . . . like he can't go out and buy a Ritz-Carlton hotel with it, but he can use it on behalf of the people.

Disagreements between Congress and the president on spending are best worked out, however, because they can cause a shutdown of the federal government. Generally that is to be avoided at all costs, except in recent years when it has been used mainly as a political gambit to demonstrate a ridiculous toughness, but it generally backfires on whichever party started the conflict.

Anyway! The budget comprises the spending limits for each category of the government that the Appropriations Committee must fund. The committee only "appropriates" the money, get it? Meaning it only decides how much each federal agency can have; it does not dispense the money or give the money out. That would be too much power for one committee to have, no checks and balances in that scenario. The "full" committee is divided into subcommittees, roughly analogous to the structure of federal departments like Commerce, Justice, Defense, Energy and Water Development, and so on. Those agencies fall under the executive branch, meaning their boss is the president.

Forgive this Civics 101 lesson, but the impact that our queen could have on that committee should not be understated. Being on the committee is like being in charge of the family piggy bank. You are not the one who decides who puts money into the bank or when, but once that bank is opened every year and the money it holds has been counted, you are the one who decides how much each member of the family will get and how much they can spend on each of their causes. And it doesn't matter how much Uncle So-and-So fusses about his portion; you make the decision. All year long, members come along on a massive scale advocating to get a larger slice of the pie.

Each of the committee's more than fifty members receives these requests. The requests have to survive a vote by a subcommittee of jurisdiction, and the full committee must decide to include them as considerations in the budget. And then that budget must have a majority vote in the full committee to be presented for a vote on the House floor.

BRENDA JONES and KRISHAN TROTMAN

As you can imagine, being involved in those early stages of the budget gives a politician a lot of power. Therefore, openings on the Appropriation Committee are sought after like *Hamilton* tickets. And they are handed out like the Academy Awards, except there are no long, teary speeches.

When Pelosi joined the Appropriations Committee, she entered a powerful club; it was as if she had been in the NCAA and now she's with the NFL. Suddenly she had even more friends, because as a member of the Appropriations Committee she would get to advocate for more money to help either their district or the areas their subcommittees represent, hence raising her popularity and street cred, giving her more power. All this love would make it much easier to get campaign contributions too.

Pelosi's placement on the Approps Committee, as it's called on the Hill, enabled her to steer spending toward priorities such as the funding for communities affected by AIDS that she became known for.

Respect for Pelosi's capability as a legislator and her willingness to skillfully stand up to presidents, whether Democratic or Republican, became notable, and she was asked to take on even more important responsibilities in the House. Appropriations is one of the prime placements, but she was also appointed a few years later to sit on the House Intelligence and Ethics Committees, which means she was privy to a lot of national and—*shhh*—personal secrets. The Intelligence

maybe *it will take* a **woman** to clean up the...

HOUSE

Committee, formally named the US House Permanent Select Committee on Intelligence, carries out some of its business behind closed doors because it oversees the CIA, the NSA, top secret intelligence operations of all the branches of the military, and any intelligence operations carried out by any department of the executive branch, such as the Departments of Defense and Justice and the Drug Enforcement Administration. Pelosi was in a position that to get a whiff of her was to smell power. She was a woman on a man's playing field but she was set, nevertheless. They had to bow to this lady.

The Committee on Ethics investigates allegations made against members of the House. Like the Intelligence Committee, it also operates often behind closed doors to protect members from false allegations. It does at times hold public actions, such as when a member of the House is censured by the House. Once she joined this committee, Pelosi knew where all the proverbial bodies were buried. It made her quite a force to be reckoned with and she knew it.

Throughout all this time, keep in mind that Pelosi had to run again to claim her seat every two years, and she still has to do it to this day. That's the thing about the House: it's hard to get too comfortable. The framers designed it so that in order to stay there, each member would have to make a direct appeal to the people every two years.

Suffice it to say, despite the fact that leadership was not her ambition when she first set foot on the Hill, she came to see its value and realized she was in a position to grab the brass ring. She didn't seek it, but when she became aware that she was in a good place to win strategically, she made a run for it. Hey, girl, who wouldn't?

And once she knew the time had come for her to step up even further, Pelosi said in a conversation portrayed in *Madam Speaker*, "Being in leadership strengthens your hand in every issue you are involved with. You are more than a member. Anything you are interested in becomes more important. Anything you say is important because you are a leader."

Pelosi would continue to reign.

BORN TO WIN

Baby, how you feeling?
Feeling good as hell.
—Lizzo, "Good as Hell"

ancy Pelosi didn't make public her ambition to become the first female Speaker of the House. Mainly, she kept it to herself. The guys might never see her coming because they tended to underestimate a woman, and she could use that to her advantage. However, the moves she was making signaled the potential that she might want to do more. Her name was thrown into the mix in all kinds of leadership discussions, including as a vice-presidential nominee, but she thought her liberal politics were not a suitable match to a political climate that was growing more and more conservative. Plus, she liked thinking for herself, not conforming to the ideas of a president, which is what a vice president is supposed to do.

No, what appealed to her, on the *low*, was the role of Speaker of the House.

Let's back up for a second, girlfriend. Just to be sure we're all on the same page, here are the basics about what it means to be Speaker of the House. First, it means you're in charge of the House and its proceedings. That means swearing in new members, presiding over the chamber (aka wielding that gavel like a *boss*), running the steering committee, which assigns party members to House committees, and more. Being Speaker means you're the top dog of your party, which, historically, has been the majority party—getting elected requires a majority of the House vote, so it's always worked that way. Ranking below the Speaker in the party, in order, are the Majority Leader, the Majority Whip, the Assistant Speaker, and the party's Caucus Chairman. (All of those except Assistant Speaker have counterparts in the minority party.) The Speaker of the House is also next in line for the presidency, after the vice president.

Basically, it's an immensely powerful position that favors those who think strategically—and when Pelosi first started thinking about it, only men had ever held that gavel. Men who tended to be remembered, either for their greatness or the harm they could cause with all that power. Men like Tip O'Neill, who retired after a long tenure just a few months before Pelosi's election; he was beloved by his colleagues and renowned for his generosity and dedication to good government. Or like Newt Gingrich, who became Speaker in 1995 at the peak of a polarizing career—*he* might be best known for leading the impeachment proceedings against President Clinton and generally sending decorum in American politics down the drain.

So sure, vice president of the United States is a prestigious title, but in Pelosi's mind, Speaker was the right role for her, if the opportunity were to present itself.

And in order to be Speaker one day, first she had to become the whip.

Pelosi's penchant for class and decorum made it unlikely she would ever show the hand of her ambition. She would never be so indiscreet. But the seas parted when a member of the California delegation, Rep. Vic Fazio, decided to retire. Pelosi was loyal to her delegation. As long as there was even a chance that Fazio might jump into the ring, she declared there was no vacancy for the whip position. But once Fazio decided to retire, Pelosi began to listen to colleagues who supported her. She kept raising millions of dollars for candidates throughout the Democratic Party, and her allies began to ask her to consider what she was getting in return. More and more money was essential to winning a campaign, as the cost of congressional, gubernatorial, and even mayoral races began to soar into the millions to win. The one person who was sure to pull that off would be her!

Television ads cost big bucks, especially before the advent of cable, when the whole nation still watched three major broadcast channels. Getting on those airwaves was increasingly the only way to win. Pelosi's ability to raise money remained important to her relationships with members who had relied on her for that cash.

What attracted her most about leadership was the way she could help push her agenda forward. In the years that she had been in Congress, Democrats were losing elections, and loose cannons had taken over the House and sought to change the relationship of the federal government to the people. They were portraying it as a "broken" institution, when they were the ones breaking it.

The tide was turning, not because the government was broken, but because wealthy interests felt they had less power over government than before. Plus, the wealth of the federal government was so great, some private interests wanted those billions of federal dollars to be privatized so they could benefit and not have to suffer federal oversight. Pelosi was interested in gaining more authority so she could make a dent in these injustices. Don't get it wrong: she believed in compromise and knew many of the rich, but she did not believe in unfair advantage gained through discriminatory practices, or deregulation that invited damage to the environment and to labor, animal, or voting rights. She wanted a chance in the center ring to see if her leadership could make a difference and keep that turning tide from rolling back fifty years.

She began to host dinners at her new spacious condo in Georgetown, and to talk to members on the phone and determine whether she might have the votes to win. Her main opponent was an old friend from Maryland whom she had first met in Senator Brewster's office years before, Rep. Steny Hoyer. Hoyer had become a top aide for Brewster and then ran for Congress himself. This was his second attempt at whip.

Sis, Hoyer was the golden boy—he had maintained several leadership positions as co-chair of the Democratic Steering Committee and chief candidate recruiter for the Democratic Congressional Campaign Committee. He was a moderate who promised to be the peacemaker who would lead the party in working more progressively with the GOP. On the other hand, Pelosi was liberal yet reasonable, and a reliable woman among a band of men. But to go as far as to ask for a leadership position on that level? Couldn't she just be happy with the seat she already had?

Hoyer was well liked and articulate and was often referred to as a "member's member," the archetypal member of Congress, a portrait of old-boy politics. While he was at the University of Maryland, and back when Pelosi's father had served in Congress, Hoyer made the trips to Big Tommy's house to pay his respects and ask for his support. He had entered politics early and become a senator in Maryland at age twenty-seven. He too had served on the Appropriations Committee; they had both worked at Brewster's office. He considered Pelosi a friend.

The issue was they both wanted to be whip, and there could only be one.

It wasn't a problem for Pelosi. Of course it wouldn't be for her.

It *was* a problem for Hoyer.

He had the confidence of the old-boys' club; most members thought whip or Speaker would likely happen for him one day. So it was plain odd to him when he got the phone call. As Pelosi began to assess that she had a chance at whip, she just called Hoyer on the phone and told him directly that she intended to run. **mic drop**

He was stunned, confused. When he ran for whip in 1991 and lost—Pelosi had been the one to second his nomination. When he got the call that this time she'd be running *against* him—his vibe was like, "Huh?"

Of course, Hoyer remained collegial. But he knew he had a formidable adversary on his hands and that Pelosi would never have called him had she not known she had the votes. He'd known her for forty years and he knew that there could be blood in this fight. She usually got what she wanted and only threw a punch she'd land.

Pelosi asked her lieutenants to shore up parts of the caucus that might tend to stray. John Murtha, a labor leader from Pennsylvania, had not been on the Hill for long. She dispatched him to remind the "old bulls" of the House of their loyalty to her father, whom some had served with years before. She engaged a conservative Democratic group from the California delegation, called the Blue Dogs, to do her bidding among that branch of the party. Part of her advocacy for herself was to suggest that the Democratic Party needed to promote a woman to a leadership position. She felt that the sooner people saw a woman in leadership, the sooner they would be willing to accept a woman as president.

By this point, presidents had put several women in leadership positions—Clinton made Madeleine Albright the first female secretary of state and Alexis Herman labor secretary. It was time, Pelosi felt, for the leadership of Congress to signal that it too recognized the capacity of women to lead. She began her campaign for whip early, but when the Republicans held on to their majority in the House in 2000, she knew she would have to wait another two years. She also knew she wanted a place in leadership to help identify strategic party actions that seemed to right the wayward course of electoral politics in America. Pelosi counted votes with the best of them.

She was surprised at the outcome of the presidential election in 2000, the "hanging chad" election that was finally certified by the Supreme Court. Research later revealed the undercounting in Florida, and even at the time the curious failure of voting machines was evident—and it made Pelosi want a crack at leadership even more. Clearly, something was terribly wrong. Funny counting of votes was not unheard-of in American history, but she had never seen anything so blatant. She wanted a seat at the table, an opportunity to defend the party she had served all her life against a new wave that was not democracy at its best, but instead a victory for the worst impulses in America.

From her standpoint, Democrats were winning elections in the west, especially in the state of California. Why weren't they winning elsewhere in the country?

She felt that as party whip, she would have to be heard. And she could use her skill to win some victories for the party, which had been routed in recent elections and had to suffer the impeachment of Bill Clinton. She wanted a crack at the top.

"For a long time, a woman in any arena has to always kind of say, 'Listen to me, hear me.' Now I'll be in a place where, ipso facto, just by virtue of the office, just by dint of what I'm doing and the position I hold . . . people will listen."

She wanted to make change, innovative change. She was feelin' the sparks rising from the internet boom in Silicon Valley, the heat of pure genius that was charging the air on the West Coast. Dynamic change was occurring, but she felt a "wall of resistance" when she came back to Washington, a regressive tendency to rely on stereotypes and old ideas to frame the circumstances of the twenty-first century. She wanted to bring a sense of *fresh to def* to the traditions of politics, sis. Perhaps she could help turn the tide. It would be dope to make history, to be the first woman whip.

She had already become the first female ranking member of the Intelligence Committee. She wanted to break the marble ceiling, not only to gain power for herself but also to combat everything that she had endured: the doubts about her capability, the incredulous looks people gave her when she told them she was in charge, that she had the plan, she had implemented it, and she had hit the mark.

She wanted to break through once and for all and let the world know, the time for women in leadership had finally come. And that's exactly what she did.

It was a tightly competitive race between her and Hoyer that had the entire Democratic caucus anxiously counting votes. Even though the leadership races are conducted in secret, Pelosi went so far as to release her list of promised voters—one hundred in all whom she declared were unequivocal in their support . . . or at least were on notice that they needed to be.

On the day of the vote, her camp was a guerrilla operation, giving aides a 7:30 A.M. wake-up call, and if anyone needed a car ride over to the Capitol Building to vote, they'd pick them up. The calls went out even to those who lived just a few blocks away! She called all of her one hundred pledged supporters. She served breakfast for members before the vote, not taking any chances of low-blood-sugar slip-ups.

Pelosi assured members of Congress that she was after the whip post to make sure legislative power and instruction were handled correctly. She promised that she'd make their votes count just as much as the leadership's—that, under her, their voices would be heard. She had donated $1 million to their campaigns, and had been a top congressional contributor. When Pelosi spoke at the caucus meeting, she promised them that she would showcase the talent among the Democratic members and that "with my election we will make history and we will make progress and we will win back the House." They trusted that Nancy Pelosi had their back. Once the last ballot box was opened, it was official. She had made history.

She was the minority whip—118 to 95.

The next morning her predecessor, David Bonior, before setting off for his retirement, gave Pelosi a black leather whip. *smile* A sweet symbol for a trailblazer, and an obvious political Dom.

In a television interview the day after she was sworn in, she said, "Over two hundred years of our history, no woman has ever risen to these heights in the Congress of the United States. No woman has gone to the White House in the capacity of senior, in a senior position in the Congress to sit at the table with the president, to discuss the issues facing our country and the president's agenda. And so it's pretty exciting."

Pelosi did it, y'all. She broke the marble ceiling, and things could never be the same again. It is reported that when Republicans heard she won over Hoyer, they cheered—they planned to use her liberalism and West Coast address against her and the Democrats. It would be a fight to the death, and it still isn't over.

★

THE WHIP

Pay no attention to them haters
Because we whip 'em off.
—Willow Smith, "Whip My Hair"

he whip. It sounds like a seductive job title. But the term is actually a British foxhunting reference. It derives from the *whipper-in,* the hunter who keeps the hounds from wandering and keeps all of them in a pack during a chase.

If that doesn't explain what's ahead, nothing does.

The whip is the enforcer. The one who makes sure that a congressperson has gotten their tail down to the voting session, who ensures that any wannabe legislative bad boy trying to bend the rules is actually voting in alignment with the official policies.

If you're a sheep dropping out of line from the party, it's the whip who gets you back in the fold.

If a Democratic leader has a bill on the floor, it's the whip who's expected to flex her muscle to get him the largest number of Democratic votes in support of it, and if possible bend some Republicans to her will as well.

The whip will watch over her team's every move. She is an equally skilled schmoozer and arm-twister, all in the mission of diplomacy. She'll know all of your staff's *and* even your cousin's business because she is well versed in and responsible for gaining legislative intelligence. (Everyone has a queen in their crew who *thinks* she's the whip.)

In 2001, Nancy Pelosi was selected as the House minority whip, the first woman elected in United States history to hold that position! EVER!

In her new role as whip, many considerations make up her agenda—party campaign platforms, research and polling data pertaining to certain issues, and the likelihood that a bill can pass in light of the members' opinions in the House, especially those in the majority, regardless of party. Leadership considers the priorities and needs of members—for example, if one state has experienced a major disaster and a vote is required to get that state funding, that would be a priority; or if there are mandatory deadlines for a bill that must be met to renew programs or let them die. These are the kinds of considerations that came across Pelosi's desk now. But ultimately, the majority leader decides when bills will come to the floor for a vote by the entire House.

The majority or minority whip leads an entire organization of members and staff to find out where other members stand on individual votes. If their vote will coincide with the party agenda, fine. If it does not, the whip organization will try to persuade them to change their vote. The whip organization is responsible for counting votes so that the leadership team knows exactly what the chances of passage or defeat of a bill might be, and they can strategize accordingly.

Of course, they don't go in blind ahead of each vote. The whip organization takes many factors into account when they assess the viability of a legislative vehicle. They have detailed research on each member and their district that helps them to predict how they are likely to vote on an issue. They know it all, sis.

It's all about triangulating, so they have to keep on top of things. For example, some districts, though they elected a Democrat, are quite conservative, so there are instances where those members may need to vote with their constituents and not with the party. Members who have to vote against a bill to please their district are already accounted for when the whip organization counts votes. Unless it is critical, most members are given latitude to vote according to their conscience or district, but there are times when arms must be twisted, girlfriend, to encourage members to vote the party line.

Incentives are used to encourage compliance. *Ooooh, gifts?* No, pressure.

Pressure is applied through repeated phone calls—chill, sis, they're not like the kind people receive from bill collectors. Promises are made to help them with the passage of other bills that are important to them, their district, or even their individual goals in exchange for a vote. If it is a very important vote, even spouses and BFFs can be pulled in to persuade, *mm-hmm*. Calls or visits from influential constituents also help sway them to vote in favor of party needs.

Counting votes is key because it allows leadership to plan strategically ahead of time, either to boost a bill through the Senate and to the president's desk, or to shut it down. If the count were left up to chance, then leaders would always be behind the eight ball trying to mitigate the impact of a vote after it is over. If they know the outcome before it happens, they can use the remaining time and avenues to strategize the next move after the inevitable happens. Remember, politics involves lots of moving parts, so anytime they can neutralize the impact of one variable, it makes life easier.

In addition to gaining legislative intelligence, Whip Pelosi was also responsible for maintaining party discipline, and she used her power well.

She focused in on the majority leader's agenda, which at the time was to look after workers' interests due to growing layoffs. With this clear goal, she was able to get continued cooperation and support from moderates even though she was a self-described progressive.

Her focus was to help chart a course for Democrats to re-gain control of the House. It would happen, but it would take longer than she had imagined. Patience and action are key attributes of a queen.

★

THE EDGE OF GLORY

And what I gotta say, is rebel
While today is still today, choose well.
—Lauryn Hill, "I Find It Hard to Say"

Okay, ladies, she was whip but that wasn't the end goal, remember. Pelosi was Serena in a tennis match; she had to stay focused.

Pelosi did not remain whip for long. She had already calculated that if Democrats won the majority in 2002, Dick Gephardt, a very popular centrist Democrat, either would become Speaker, which would allow her to move up to the role of majority leader, or might run for president of the United States.

As whip, she made good on her promises. She helped Democrats far and wide, embracing the big-tent nature of her party, even the more centrist Blue Dog coalition that had formed in the past decade. Pelosi understood the Blue Dogs' criticisms and helped them raise money, but she believed that ultimately her more liberal ideals would win the day.

Pelosi spent just over a year as minority whip. In 2003, she was elected to lead the Democrats as minority leader. She was sixty-two years old and was in her ninth term as a representative of San Francisco. She also went on to hold her ground in the 2004 election, but now what sparked her leadership was that as minority leader, she was able to help craft the strategy of the 2006 midterm election, where the Democrats would go on to gain thirty seats—ending twelve years of Republican dominance in the chamber.

But even before that wave election, she had reason to be proud. After 214 years in a two-party congressional system, finally the country was seeing its first woman minority leader of a political party.

AS MINORITY LEADER, Pelosi was confused by the Bush administration's war agenda of ridding Iraq of weapons of mass destruction. She was a member of the Intelligence Committee and therefore saw for herself the bulk of information that was gathered—at least what the executive branch could let them see—and there was no evidence that the United States was in imminent danger, as Bush claimed. *sigh* Did Bush know something that no one else knew? No. Simple: Pelosi voted against the war. *mic drop*

She was outspoken about it, and certain GOP members

didn't like that. Thus began a fight between Pelosi and Bush that would continue throughout his presidency.

Ahead of the 2004 election, Bush was searching for a reason to be liked again. *snicker* One of his big ideas was to reform and privatize Social Security. (Oh. My. God. Stop.) Minority Leader Pelosi's takedown of this idea would showcase her in the public eye on a new level. It was a next-level slay. After she succeeded, her colleagues and the media recognized that her strengths reached far beyond her talent for fundraising. Yep, unfortunately that was still in question??? They understood now that she was a real *boss* who saved our country from a Social Security crisis.

It was only her second year as party leader, but Pelosi still had the audacity to instruct party members to strike down Bush's request. He was cruisin' like D'Angelo around the country—from coast to coast, but mainly in the red states—promoting his new big idea for Social Security. The concept was that private accounts would replace Social Security retirement benefits. Republicans held the majority in the House, so he didn't see why this big idea wouldn't happen or couldn't happen. The problem was he didn't have a plan for rolling it out or how it would work long-term. *Oy!* He expected everyone else to figure that part out.

Under Pelosi's leadership, the Dems weren't having it. They brass-knuckled the idea as much as they could—hosting town hall meetings and doing whatever else they could to get the constituents fired up. Bush argued that Social Security was in crisis and privatization would help. Dems argued that putting the country's retirement savings at the mercy of the market would make things worse. Many people were depending on Social Security in their retirement plans, and it wasn't worth the risk.

Bush had been high on his reelection and a new era of Republican policy making since they dominated the House throughout his term, so he figured Congress could work out the details. They had already passed major legislation in terms of authorizing the Iraq War, tax cuts, and Medicare reform—they had gotten this all done with Democratic votes. But the way Bush had handled Iraq and was now treating Social Security was increasingly exasperating to his own party. The Republicans could have backed him on Social Security reform, but they couldn't reach a consensus on how to achieve his goal.

To flip the script, they tried to push the issue onto the Democrats' table. *Well, if you don't like the new plan, then do something about it. Ha! Think of something better, smarty-pants.* When they asked Minority Leader Pelosi when her party would present a new plan, her famous words were "Never. Is never good enough for you?"

The way she saw it, Social Security was a plan that was already working, and why fix what isn't broken?

Social Security is like highlighter on our US citizenship. And why was Bush trying to give up responsibility for this cash flow for seniors and privatize it? Yes, the future of Social Security is still an issue, but we must improve it, not dismantle it, was Pelosi's reasoning. While she was comfortable in her adult life, she was raised in an immigrant community in Little Italy, where common folks worked their tails off knowing that the government had plans and respect for their hard work, and they would be taken care of in their old age. Think about it: Pelosi herself was eligible for retirement when Bush started talking this sh*t. She must've been furious.

Thankfully, Bush's master plan went nowhere quick. Under Pelosi's will, it evaporated into space. No one with any real juice has tried to come for Social Security since.

* * * * * * * * ★ * * * * * * * *

QUEEN

Where we can find
our common ground,
we shall seek it. Where
we cannot find that
common ground, we
must stand our
ground.

—NANCY PELOSI, PRESS CONFERENCE,
JANUARY 26, 2003

MADAM SPEAKER

R-E-S-P-E-C-T
Find out what it means to me.
—Aretha Franklin, "Respect"

t's 2006, and the House Democrats have finally won back the majority after twelve long years thanks to Pelosi. Suddenly she's Snow White, but with hundreds of dwarfs, and they're off to work, off to a new adventure, a new Congress for 2007! Pelosi helped to engineer the Dems' takeover. After four years as the leader of Democrats in the minority, and at sixty-six years old, she became the highest-ranked woman ever in government, second to vice president Dick Cheney and President George W. Bush.

Rep. John Boehner of Ohio handed over the gavel after she beat him 233 to 202 and became Speaker of the House for the 110th Congress. She wore a wine-colored suit and gold jewelry, making bae look like the heart of the Democratic Party. She stood before a crowd of cheering men and women, surrounded by her grandchildren and generations old and new. She gave a queenly wave, kindly sending Boehner into the back as the new minority leader, and he praised her as he should, acknowledging and celebrating her as the first woman ever elected for the position.

Speaker Pelosi stepped up to the mic as cheers of "Nancy" echoed through the House. She *served* them some soaring rhetoric:

> *It's a historic moment for the Congress. It's a historic moment for the women of America. It's a moment for which we have waited over two hundred years.*
>
> *Never losing faith, we waited through the many years of struggle to achieve our right. But women weren't just waiting, women were working.*
>
> *Never losing faith, we worked to redeem the promise of America that all men and* women *are created equal.*
>
> *For our daughters and our granddaughters today, we have broken the marble ceiling.*
>
> *For our daughters and our granddaughters now, the sky is the limit.*
>
> *Anything is possible for me. . . .*

In true Pelosi fashion, she also laid the groundwork right away for what she would stand for as Speaker. Any good leader knows that the first step is to establish who you are and what you represent right away. The new Speaker said, "I

MADAM
SPEAKER

accept this gavel in the spirit of partnership, not partisanship." She also joked that after handing over the gavel for the last two Congresses, she was happy to have Boehner do the honors this time. This time her party had won. She thanked her husband and children for "the confidence they gave me to go from the kitchen to the Congress." She said that the 2006 election was marking a way forward and represented a new vision of Congress. She said that she was committed to disentangling US troops from the war in Iraq. The Dems' agenda was to increase the minimum wage, cut the interest rates on federal student loans, and end a number of subsidies to big oil companies.

Her first rule of order was to "pass the toughest congressional ethics reform in history." This was a response to the scandals of the Republican-led 109th Congress. Pelosi would limit lobbyists' ability to entertain members or their staffs, and reinstate the "pay as you go" rules for the federal budget, which would require that any new spending "be offset by spending cuts or increased taxes." PAYGO adds some control over the budget so fools aren't throwing government cash in the air like they're in a Fat Joe video, and increases control of deficit spending.

And she was really specific, people: "This new Congress doesn't have two years or two hundred days; let us join together in the first one hundred hours to make this the most honest and open Congress in history. First one hundred hours." First one hundred hours?! Madam Speaker was already establishing herself as a queen who could turn *up*. Who talks like that? We know that there are twenty-four hours in one day, but no one else is counting hours like Pelosi. During the first one hundred legislative hours, beginning on a Tuesday, she promised to have votes after being sworn in on Thursday. Then, also in typical Pelosi fashion, she invited all the children present to join her onstage and told them and her grandchildren to touch the gavel. *Yasss*, girl!

The House. Will. Come. To. Order. *Boom!*

THE HUNDRED-HOUR PLAN was a play on President Franklin Roosevelt's promise during the Great Depression to take quick action during his first hundred days in office. Speaker Pelosi's hundred hours proposal referred to one hundred business hours, or the legislative time available prior to the president's 2007 State of the Union address a few weeks later.

Again, Pelosi is infamously good at math. **smile** By January 18, 2007, *eighty-seven* business hours after she was sworn in, the Democratic-led House under Speaker Pelosi had passed every proposal she pledged to make.

Pelosi's aide said, "People have lost their career underestimating Nancy Pelosi. They mistake her patience for complacency, kindness for competitive instinct, and a willingness to share credit with not holding the reins tightly."

In eighty-seven legislative hours, the House voted to raise the minimum wage, gave the green light on funded embryonic stem-cell research, implemented recommendations for the 9/11 Commission, cut oil and gas tax breaks, empowered Medicare to negotiate drug-price discounts, *and* cut student loan rates. With poll-tested legislation, the bill passed and the Dems recruited sixty-two Repubs to join in for the vote. Pelosi hit the ground like a champion sprinter, and she carried her party over the finish line. Her campaign slogan had been "A New Direction," and within less than the time she allotted herself, she was already *laying it down*! Democrats fulfilled their "Six of '06" agenda.

We're just gonna imagine that Bush was tossing and turning in his sleep in January when she won the race for Speaker. *Bwahaha*. His battle with Pelosi and now Majority Leader Harry Reid over the handling of the Iraq War was just beginning.

★

BAD ROMANCE

I want your love, and I want your revenge.
You and me could write a bad romance.
—Lady Gaga, "Bad Romance"

So, let's keep it 100: Speaker Pelosi thought George W. Bush was trash. It's fine, everyone has a coworker like George. She called him "incompetent," "dangerous," "a liar," "a total failure," and declared him "The Emperor with No Clothes" and who-knows-what-else when talking behind closed doors to her darling husband, Paul. Let's be honest. "The president led us into the Iraq War on the basis of unproven assertions without evidence. He embraced a radical doctrine of preemptive war unprecedented in our history, and he failed to build a true international coalition," she said at the 2004 State of the Union address. Basically, he had screwed the pooch on the war and the threat of WMDs and the economy. "Therefore, American taxpayers are bearing almost all the cost: a colossal $120 billion and rising. More importantly, American troops are enduring almost all the casualties: tragically, five hundred killed and thousands more wounded."

They had their moments, though. In 2008, even with a divided House, Bush signed bills that dealt with AIDS relief, taxes, and energy. In 2007, Pelosi worked with him to increase the federal minimum wage by attaching it to the Iraq War spending. She figured, if we have to pay for this foolish war, we might as well sneak in some progressive gains. In 2009 the minimum wage increased from $5.15 per hour to $7.25. (The problem: as of this writing, a decade later, it's still $7.25.)

She also brought the caucus together on bailing out the banks during the 2008 financial collapse. But there was also tons of *drama*. Take, for example, a famous meeting she attended with Sen. Harry Reid, the Bush administration, and the two presidential candidates, to make sure that the government wasn't going to just hand the big banks a fat check at the expense of the everyday people. The Democratic demands were "to add stimulus to provide financial relief for American families who had just seen their savings wiped out, restricting so-called golden parachutes for bank CEOs, and requiring banks and other institutions that received bailout money to eventually pay it back to taxpayers—with interest." Well, Bush was just being conniving and confusing to everyone, honey—even fellow Republicans were growing impatient with his indecision and lack of leadership skills. Obama was there. John McCain was there. They were both running for president and this was the example being set! The meeting was a sham, and that's about all they agreed on. Pelosi, Obama, and McCain left. Irritated, Pelosi was trying to get in some post-strategy remarks in the Roosevelt Room when Bush's treasury secretary, Henry Paulson, ran in like a desperate suitor. He literally got down on one knee to beg Speaker Pelosi not to give up on the talks, and to "help save the country from financial ruin."

"Don't blow this up," he said. What?! Why is a man always putting all the weight on a woman? *Cue Lizzo: "Why men great till they gotta be great?"* She wasn't the president. Shouldn't he be talking to Bush?

Still, the moment showed how strong Pelosi's record was in working with Democratic and Republican presidents. Suddenly this guy was dependent on *her*! *Where's your testosterone-laden, war-starting, enemy-killing steroid instincts now, Texas boy?* Pelosi probably wanted to ask had she not been so polite. Plus, he'd just wasted her time and everyone else's in that meeting. Now he was coming to her, not even a member of his own party, to help pick up the pieces. This *please, baby, pleeeeease* moment led to a Senate reform bill known as the Troubled Asset Relief Program making it through the House and being signed by Bush. Then, when Obama became president, he approved the $819 billion stimulus package. *Whew.*

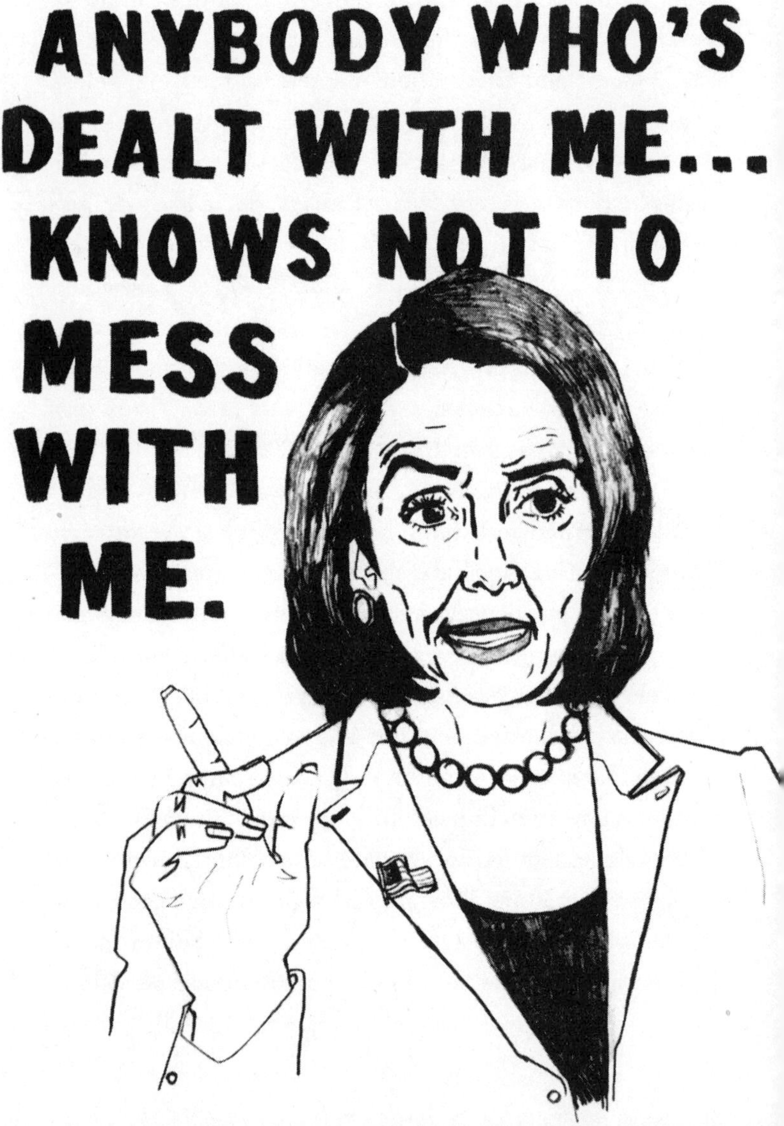
ANYBODY WHO'S DEALT WITH ME... KNOWS NOT TO MESS WITH ME.

---★---

YES, WE DID!

'Cause to be victorious,
You must find glory in the little things.
—Janelle Monáe, "Victory"

Though the worst of the financial crisis and attacks on entitlements under Bush were now a thing of the past, Pelosi and her party had another big promise to deliver on: comprehensive healthcare reform.

The truth is that most American families are at risk of going under, but they do not realize it until it's too late. The number one reason that Americans go bankrupt, as another Queen of the Resistance, Elizabeth Warren, has testified to on many occasions, is the skyrocketing cost of healthcare. This was especially true in the years leading up to 2010. All that is required in this land of the free and home of the brave is for one family member to be compromised by a catastrophic health crisis—cancer, heart disease, kidney failure, or a stroke—the leading causes of most chronic healthcare issues in this country. If just one American family member gets sick—even among middle- and professional-class families who are working, who have employer-paid health insurance—they become much more likely to slide into bankruptcy. It's not because they aren't working hard enough. It's not because they are not saving enough. It's because the cost of the treatments and medications required to overcome the disease are more expensive here than in most other countries in the world. The same drugs! The same treatments!

We've all been there: rushing to the emergency room feeling woozy and out of sorts, only to be stopped at admissions first thing to make sure our insurance will pay for whatever the hospital may have to do. Once we are discharged, we think we are fine, only to discover a few weeks later a whopping bill in the mail.

And if Americans who are working and have health insurance are more likely to go bankrupt if one family member contracts a major illness, imagine what happens to the working poor when they get hurt or sick. Waitresses, ride-share drivers, fast-food workers, part-time employees. The people who wash your car, clean your building, or manage food service at your office. The people who come in to help your elderly mom or dad, who work at the corner store, the gas station, or the dry cleaner's. Many of these people are the working poor, some with two or three jobs, most with little to no healthcare benefits. Most of these members of our community cannot afford treatment or the required prescription drugs, and so they have to delay expenditures on doctor visits and on medications, a vicious cycle that keeps many from getting well and keeps them racking up even more medical debt.

LET'S BACK UP for a minute. Workers have been fighting for some kind of comprehensive healthcare since the early 1900s. The American Medical Association had been against it for years because "it had come to see health insurance legislation as a threat to both their independence and income." So Franklin Roosevelt left universal healthcare out of his massive Social Security legislation, which lifted the elderly out of poverty, because of the medical lobby.

President Lyndon Johnson later made passing Medicare and Medicaid legislation in 1965 a key part of his War on Poverty plan. He expanded healthcare coverage to the elderly, the disabled, the widowed, and the orphaned, all of whom struggled even at 1965 prices to pay for healthcare. The measures increased the ability of people who needed healthcare to pay for it, expanding the pool of paying customers while enfranchising people who desperately needed support. It lifted people out of poverty by making the government a nonprofit health insurer. Johnson's advances, though, still did not strike at the core of the mounting healthcare crisis: that working families, regardless of income, faced financial doom, if any one of their family members ever got sick. Important steps had been made, but universal healthcare remained a dream for the future.

Decades later, when Bill Clinton's administration tried to pass healthcare reform with First Lady Hillary at the helm, she purposely left the physicians and the pharmaceutical companies out of her planning because of their long-standing history as an impediment to these goals. It looked like the only way to affect healthcare was through a piecemeal approach that bit by bit addressed the overall problems facing so many Americans. Unfortunately, even with this approach, Republicans put up such harsh opposition that the administration could not pass a successful bill.

Neither Bush administration (which came right before and after Clinton's) had any interest in expanding social welfare programs. In fact, under their leadership (and Ronald Reagan's in the 1980s) the federal government had offered several tax cuts that severely reduced the income of the federal government, restricting its capacity to engage in programs that would relieve these kinds of burdens for Americans. George W. Bush's ill-fated attempt to privatize Social Security (thank you, Nancy!) should give you an idea of how little the GOP cared about social programs.

In 2007 and 2008, as the presidential campaign heated up, Barack Obama campaigned heavily on the issue. At a Families

USA Conference in January 2007, Obama made what some consider one of his best speeches on the need for universal healthcare:

More than sixty years after President Truman first issued the call for national health insurance, we find ourselves in the midst of an historic moment on health care. From Maine to California, from business to labor, from Democrats to Republicans, the emergence of new and bold proposals from across the spectrum has effectively ended the debate over whether or not we should have universal health care in this country.

Plans that tinker and halfway measures now belong to yesterday. . . . I know there's a cynicism out there about whether this can happen, and there's reason for it. Every four years, health care plans are offered up in campaigns with great fanfare and promise. But once those campaigns end, the plans collapse under the weight of Washington politics, leaving the rest of America to struggle with skyrocketing costs.

For too long, this debate has been stunted by what I call the smallness of our politics—the idea that there isn't much we can agree on or do about the major challenges facing our country. And when some try to propose something bold, the interests groups and the partisans treat it like a sporting event, with each side keeping score of who's up and who's down, using fear and divisiveness and other cheap tricks to win their argument, even if we lose our solution in the process. . . . It's time to act. This isn't a problem of money, this is a problem of will. A failure of leadership.

No wonder this guy was elected by a landslide.

All of that sounded very good, but the truth is it became much easier said than done. Still, it was whipping up hope (pun intended) in so many different corners of American life. Pelosi felt it. Passing a healthcare-reform bill would be one of the greatest moments for the Democratic Party in recent memory. It was one of the biggest pieces of social legislation in decades. Not since Social Security and Medicaid and Medicare had America seen such powerful legislation passed. Who better to have at the helm of that effort than Madam Pelosi?

We all know now that the Affordable Care Act made it through, but the story of how the Democrats pulled it off is equipped with a good dose of juicy drama, sis.

BEFORE WE GET into Pelosi's role in passing the ACA, here's a clear picture of what the heck was going on with Obama and the Republicans. The sort of drama unfolding in American politics when a Black man was in charge probably had

First Lady Michelle Obama's blood boiling when she witnessed her husband being played.

Truth: At the top of his game, Barack Obama was a six-foot-one handsome Black Harvard alumnus, oozing charm and intelligence, who not only had been a star basketball player but also ran the school paper. Jocks and bookworms alike loved him, honey. Obama had all those bases covered, but in a confrontational dome like Capitol Hill, there was bound to be trouble. It didn't help that Obama represented a serious blip on the opposition radar.

For years, even during the Clinton administration, conservatives in Congress were working on getting rid of social programs and progressive presidents. Up until the 2006 election that launched Pelosi into the Speaker's chair, they had enjoyed years of Republican majority and tax cut after tax cut that hampered federal ability to pay for social programs, and put more and more money into corporate coffers and bank accounts.

Then, out of the blue, here comes Barack Obama, swooping in with a plan to give some power back to the people, a goal totally opposed to what the Republicans were doing. They wanted private enterprise to manage all of society's problems, regardless of the cost to consumers. It didn't matter that the government could do it cheaper. Healthcare reform took a for-profit possibility out of their hands. It *had* to be defeated.

LUCKILY OBAMA HAD a secret weapon: Nancy Pelosi, the Speaker of the House. Obama has said himself that he could not have achieved anything in Congress without one important partner: "Nancy Pelosi has been that partner," he said looking back, at a conference in 2018. Obama and Pelosi spoke each other's language. She had spent a lot of her career holding back the onslaught of a hungry opposition that wanted to destroy advances that put power and federal dollars in the hands of the people. When Pelosi became Speaker, she got in there thinking that she was going to do a kind of good work.

Now, for the first time in almost thirty years, when there was a Democratic majority in the House and the Senate, and a charismatic Democrat in the White House, she felt they had to make an end run toward comprehensive healthcare reform. It was complicated, yes. People might not understand its significance in the moment. But whether people realized it or not, it was the change that would make the most dramatic difference in their lives. Americans were spending trillions on healthcare. If the Democrats could help alleviate some of the cost of healthcare, it would help preserve American families and put resources back in their pockets. It was a great opportunity to achieve progress, not fight against regressive policies.

Obama was in, but the advisers around him were already concerned about his chances at reelection. They were worried that this particular struggle would expend too much of the political capital he had earned through an unprecedented win and positive energy worldwide. He had earned a Nobel Peace Prize before even lifting a finger as president because the committee felt that if America could set aside centuries of grief around the issues of race and elect an African American president, his election itself sent a message of hope.

Meanwhile, Capitol Hill had sunk further into a morass of partisanship. Let's not get confused. Getting healthcare reform passed was hard because, again, Republicans had been working to cut social programs since the Reagan administration. And things tilted and spilled over congressionally rather quickly when Obama became president—we really got to see what had been on the horizon for American politics for a long time.

Many people argue that the political ugliness got its start with Newt Gingrich, when he rose to prominence in Congress in the late 1980s. He invented the modern tactic of making a scene and stirring up cultural clashes on the House floor. The Dems saw this as a political strategy; they did not realize how pervasive and subversive it really was. Years later the GOP took this tactic to a new and more personal level, with vicious attacks on the Clintons, 2004 Democratic presidential nominee John Kerry, and then Obama.

*   *   *

BACK TO HEALTHCARE. The Obama administration thought at first that they could work on the campaign by reaching across the aisle. Obama tried negotiating with Republicans, but they were totally uninterested. He tried many times to find common ground, but there was no deal that they were willing to make with him. Eventually, Obama and his team made a decision. They'd have to pass the bill with Democrats only.

This sounds simple in theory, but Pelosi and the Obama administration knew that the Dems had issues within their own caucus.

There were plenty of hearings, folks, involved in making the bill. Pelosi orchestrated the process in the House, making sure that the developing committees knew the key elements of the bill inside and out. As a leader, she'd get into the weeds and details of policy—and not all leaders or members had the skills to do this. She worked day and night, even when others encouraged her to give it up, until she was able to count up enough votes to pass the bill. If you've learned one thing about Pelosi by now, it's that she doesn't stop, and won't introduce a bill, until she has her votes securely lined up and *receipts* at the ready.

While the several committees involved in a bill of this size—Ways and Means, Energy and Commerce, Education and Workforce, Oversight and Government Reform, and Appropriations—held hearings to explore the impact of various provisions, Pelosi spent her time tirelessly talking to every Democrat who had a question or a problem with the legislation. She listened carefully to what her members had to say, and brought their feedback to the committee chairs so they could work on solutions.

The more conservative Blue Dogs were concerned about the costs that the legislation would create. But Pelosi had answers for them on that: mainly by taxing the rich, her team had found a way to offset the expenses that would result from the Affordable Care Act. There were also concerns among more conservative Democrats that part of the bill allowed private insurance to pay for abortion care. Pelosi was able to convince the Catholic Bishops of America and others that they just couldn't compromise on this, recognizing that to do so would limit crucial rights of bodily autonomy.

Years later, Cecile Richards, longtime president of Planned Parenthood and former Pelosi staffer, remembered this moment. "I will never forget the meeting with her, when I was at Planned Parenthood, where she told me in the middle of that fight that she would not pass the Affordable Care Act if it banned insurance coverage for abortions. Though many 'progressive' men were willing to throw women under the bus, she was not." She did have to allow for the Hyde Amendment, which restricts state-funded programs like Medicaid from covering abortion care; it was a flawed solution, but choice was preserved for a vast number of people.

Meanwhile, Pelosi was also criticized by progressives who wished the law would include a public option, meaning a government-run insurance program that would compete with private carriers. Nancy wanted this as well, and she had fought for it in the months leading up to the final vote. But eventually she recognized that she couldn't get the votes to make it happen.

Obama had studied the issue, and he knew that universal healthcare was the best outcome. But he and Pelosi both knew that in such a hostile environment, it would be ripped to shreds. During that time a lot of people relied on this mantra: "Don't let the perfect be the enemy of the good." Even though Obama had campaigned in favor of big reform, they decided to go big but take universal healthcare off the table.

Pelosi was ultimately able to settle this issue with the progressives in her caucus because they knew the history of the fight. They knew she was right about the issues getting support, and that refusing to back down could jeopardize the entire bill—and then no one would get help. It was in their best interest to flow with this bill, and Pelosi assured them that, as with other government policies, they could continue to tweak the bill for years to come. For the time being, getting the work started was the most important thing. So the progressives jumped on the wagon too.

Though there were many disagreements, all of these compromises resulted in a bill they could pass with the Democratic majority. The overall model was based on the statewide Massachusetts plan that Republican governor Mitt Romney had created. On some level, Obama's team still wanted to reach across the aisle: starting with a familiar setup could help the GOP see that they were acting in good faith. Of course, Dems were giving Pelosi the side-eye up and down, but they knew it was a tactic, and if they went into the conversation with a more left-leaning bill, it would fail, and there would be millions of people still left without coverage.

It became clear that there would be no Republican support for healthcare reform anyway; they wanted to stop the bill at all costs. Lord help them, if another piece of Democratic legislation actually did succeed. The GOP was trying to *cut* social programs, not expand them. They knew that if the American people were all excited about the changes to their lives that the Affordable Care Act would bring, the bill could pass. Then they'd have to live with this thing, yikes!

So, they responded to the Democrats' good-faith negotiations with withering attacks. They twisted everything about the bill to make it seem like it would allow the government to reach into people's lives and tell them what to do. Presidential hopeful Sarah Palin helped gin up opposition by spreading untruths about "death panels" that would convene to determine whether Grandma lives or dies. It was a monster made out of a provision that allowed insurance to pay for palliative care and guidance given to terminally ill patients. Their tactic was to force the bill into a situation where people would view it as nonviable and even scary.

How could the opponents of healthcare so willingly lie and make up outrageous claims when they knew just like every other member of Congress how Americans were suffering? How could they so flagrantly sacrifice the financial security of millions of American families for a handful of wealthy people?

For some members, the idea of public service had gone out the window. They also used every trick in the book to make people think that Barack Obama was the cause of everything wrong in America. That he was the reason the economy wasn't recovering as fast as people wanted it to, not that the financial industries had been deregulated under the Bush administration. They made the link even clearer by rebranding the ACA bill as "Obamacare"—this way, it would be even easier for people to conflate their distrust of the Black, Democratic president with the bill itself. Obama flipped the script by embracing the name, saying, "I have no problem with people saying Obama cares. I do care." Still, the divisive approach nearly worked.

There were waves of attacks, and protests in front of the White House and on Capitol Hill. Some seemed volatile enough to become violent. During one protest on the Hill, during voting for the bill, Pelosi grabbed the hands of Rep. John Lewis and they formed a chain of Democratic members who walked across the street to the Capitol to vote. They sang "We Shall Overcome." The crowd was unsettled and hostile. One member of Congress was spat on. Two others were called racist and homophobic names.

The Obama White House got to a point where they wondered whether their struggle was worth it. But Pelosi convinced them to soldier on so they could score a win for the American people. She worked day and night, even when others encouraged her to give it up, until she was able to count up enough votes to pass the bill. She remained intensely focused on the long view, the goal of delivering relief for millions of Americans. And ya know what? She got those votes.

On March 25, 2010, more than three hundred lawmakers and their guests gathered in the East Room of the White House. They were smiling. They'd just come down from a roller coaster that they had been on for a year. Finally, finally they could breathe. It was over. The Affordable Care Act had been passed. Hooray! The room was alive with applause, and the feeling of accomplishment and a job well done shot through the roof. These members of Congress were *lit* with enthusiasm like a house party thrown by Kid 'n Play. *"The roof, the roof is on fire!"*

Obama entered with Vice President Joe Biden, and the crowd chanted, *"Fired up! Ready to go!"* which had been their

call-and-response throughout the process. In another room, not too far away, were five hundred more cheering people: the doctors, nurses, patients, and federal employees whom Obama was going out to meet afterward to blaze the fire, rally the people, and campaign on behalf of the good news of the bill.

Then Nancy Pelosi entered, and the cheers erupted even more loudly. The room shook as they chanted for their champion in the fight: *"Nancy! Nancy! Nancy!"* She had kept them on that roller coaster, even when they wanted to jump off. She kept the tribe together through every hair-raising turn, and there had been many. She had held them up when they felt sick with discouragement. She told them, "No, we won't stop," and kept them going and going even when they could not see a way to achieve the reforms Congress had been working on in one form or another for nearly one hundred years. *Yasss, they did it!*

THOSE GOOD VIBES, sadly, were not to last: the Republicans used their vitriolic approach, especially around healthcare, to take back the House in the 2010 election. Minority Leader Mitch McConnell even infamously declared that the goal of the Republican Party was to make Obama a one-term president. *Ugh.* Two years into that first term, Nancy Pelosi lost her Speaker's gavel, and a host of her House colleagues did not return.

* * *

ON THE HILL, the change from majority to minority is dramatic. The Speaker has at least three floors of office space in the US Capitol and dozens of staff. She is able to appoint several House officials, like the clerk of the House, the parliamentarian, committee and subcommittee chairpersons, and many other roles. When Pelosi lost the speakership, all of the people she appointed had to step down, and they lost their offices too. Hundreds of staffers lost their jobs. Some of them quickly switched to roles in different offices, but with so many staff looking, there weren't enough openings to absorb them. It was a ghost town, with stacks of desks, chairs, lamps, and other office furnishings set in the hallway for weeks until the new members were installed.

Pelosi had to move to the minority leader's office, which is maybe a third of her usual ornate and beautiful space situated right off the majestic rotunda of the Capitol, with views that looked straight down the National Mall to the Washington Monument. Now she was ensconced in the hallway near the Rayburn Room. It was still in the Capitol, but who could find it, bruh?

Sixty-three of her colleagues were gone. She had known the Democrats were going to pay a price after the fight for the Affordable Care Act, but, dang, the caucus was ravaged. With their new margin of dominance, the Republicans would never have to consult Democrats to get a bill through the House. They could have their way, and they took full advantage of it.

This was during the rise of the Tea Party, a group of Republicans billed at the time as a GOP grassroots movement.

These machinations exacerbated the partisan divide, sister. Negotiation used to happen between Democrats and Republicans in the past when they both had the same goal—the public good. But public service was not the interest of these new partisan members who had shape-shifted their own tribe reminiscent of something out of *True Blood*. The debate was not between liberals and conservatives. No, these were radicals who were against the government working for the people. They wanted to ruin government. They wanted it to fail. They weren't interested in compromise; they wanted defeat. They did not care whether their opponents represented millions of people with different opinions from theirs. They had no respect for difference. It was their way or the highway.

Pelosi and her colleagues had spent decades trying to hold these forces back. But the election of 2010 ushered all of those ideas into the center of the US Congress like a bomb waiting to explode.

The Republicans used their strength in the House and their close margin in the Senate to obstruct Obama as much as they could. Their problem was that the Tea Party proved to be so recalcitrant that it undercut its own leadership. The large number of new members became a powerful factor within the Republican Conference and called themselves the Freedom Caucus. They were so unwilling to cooperate with even the simplest traditions of the House that the Republican Speaker, John Boehner, at times had to engage Pelosi and her Democrats to get the commonsense work of the House done, even though he technically had a majority without them.

The election of 2012 was a bright spot . . . well, maybe a bright dot. House Democrats won back eight seats, but they had a long, long way to go to get into the majority again.

One of the worst moments of those years started in October 2013, when Republicans in Congress held up budget proceedings mostly to target funding for the Affordable Care Act. They were so committed to fighting this bill that would help people, and had so little regard for typical Americans and the hundreds of thousands of government employees who needed their paychecks, that they shut the whole government down for sixteen days. Pelosi and her caucus were having None. Of. It.

Things weren't really much better for the GOP, though, especially Speaker Boehner: after the 2012 election especially, the Tea Party caucus turned on him. Though it had been initially funded by the Koch brothers to challenge Democrats, the Tea Party had begun to implode and challenge Republican leaders who were more fair-minded. Twenty-five members of Boehner's own caucus decided to eject him because they felt he was too willing to negotiate with Obama. In order for him to remain in his post, he would have had to ask Pelosi to cobble together Democrats to vote for him to remain as Speaker, a highly unusual move. Rather than continue to struggle with a testy group of malcontents, he decided to leave. He ultimately stepped down as Speaker and resigned from the House in 2015.

⭐

HOLD MY PEARLS

This is my fight song
Take back my life song.
—Rachel Platten, "Fight Song"

Things only got wilder from there: the Republican Party only got more extreme and obstructive after Boehner's departure, in the House and also the Senate. One of the most salient examples is when a seat opened up on the Supreme Court. When Justice Antonin Scalia died in 2016, Obama was due to appoint a justice to take his place. But McConnell and the rest of the Senate Republicans refused to even meet with Obama's nominee. Why? No sound explanation was given. This is another example of the sort of crap Obama had to deal with. Our girl Nancy wasn't going to let those shenanigans go on without comment. "Evidently it isn't enough for Republicans to merely shut down government or threaten the faith and credit of the United States of America. They must sabotage the Supreme Court too," she said, according to *The Hill*. We were all thinking it. . . .

MEANWHILE, THE UGLIEST presidential election in memory was going down. Looking back, people often ask, how did it come to this? Meaning, Trump. Well, basically, the Republicans let the age-old monsters of race-baiting, misogyny, violence, and hostility out to play, all so they could hold on to power and complete this scheme they had to disenfranchise average Americans and empower the almighty rich. It was a Pandora's box, and the Republican Party couldn't put its own monsters to sleep.

At first, no one took Donald Trump seriously. But it didn't take long for people to realize that it was the perfect time for Trump, a supposed billionaire white man with a big mouth. As early as 2011, he had been an infamous part of the apparatus trying to delegitimize the Obama administration. His main tactic: challenging whether Obama had been born within the United States, and therefore whether his presidency was legitimate. *sigh* But with these reality-show theatrics, and by being the biggest jerk in the room—insulting every group of people aside from white men, attacking people on Twitter, inciting violence at his rallies, you name it—he became the Republican nominee. He was hired! (Well, technically not yet, but, ugh, he was the host of *The Apprentice*.) Trump represented the culmination of a looming threat that had been growing and was reminiscent of what Pelosi first encountered when she got to Congress, when Newt Gingrich was starting to introduce an openly ugly, combative side to Republican politics.

We all know what happened next. A Russian hack of the DNC's emails, some shady meetings, and a questionable press conference from FBI head James Comey later, Hillary Clinton won a majority of the popular vote but did not win enough Electoral College votes to win the presidency. And that's where Pelosi, once more the Speaker of the House, would take center stage in getting that guy out of office one way or another.

In many ways, Trump was the ultimate embodiment of the boys' club that didn't take Pelosi seriously from the jump, the ones she surprised again and again until she made it to the top. As House minority leader under the Trump administration, she had her work cut out for her.

There were a series of issues that Pelosi had with the president, of course, but work for the nation still had to get done. Though the Republicans were in control of the House, they still weren't getting much past Pelosi's agenda. Trump has said many things about her, but it didn't scare her. "I think I have my pluses and my minuses," she said in a 2019 interview in *Time*. "But I have a confidence about what I bring to the table in terms of my network . . . And I get things done, even with a Republican president."

During his first year in office, she kept her caucus in line, making sure not a single Democrat voted for Trump's huge billionaire tax cuts or his attempt to repeal the Affordable Care Act. In September 2017, she and Senate minority leader Chuck Schumer famously talked Trump into signing off on a spending deal favorable to Democrats.

At the same time, Deputy Attorney General Rod Rosenstein appointed Robert Mueller to figure out what exactly happened with the 2016 election and the firing of James Comey. It looked an awful lot like Trump had colluded with a foreign government to destroy the candidacy of Hillary Clinton. The Democrats were ringing the alarm about this to the American people, while the Republicans tried to downplay it and basically say "it's a bunch of sour grapes" and "those Dems are just sorry that they lost to our guy Trump" and "they just didn't like him, they'll say anything. They're desperate." But Minority Leader Pelosi was clearheaded; if she could take back the House with her caucus, she'd be in a position to call for impeachment if the Mueller investigation's findings, or some other scandal, warranted it.

In the meantime, she had day-to-day issues to attend to, and a few big moments of her own.

It was a Wednesday morning, 10:04 A.M., on February 7, 2018, when Pelosi took matters into her own hands as the House considered a budget proposal that contained no solution for people living under the Deferred Action for Childhood Arrivals program (DACA). She took the floor in a white

blazer, navy-blue blouse, and four-inch heels to make her one-minute speech . . . but that one minute turned into more than eight hours!

It was a strategic move on Pelosi's part to Trump and anyone else opposed to the legislation. Filibusters, unauthorized prolonged speeches, had been banned in the House long ago; the ban was meant to prevent members in the minority party from slowing things down in a debate. The odds against them forced minority parties to be creative, and Minority Leader Nancy Pelosi knew what was up. Leadership can technically take unlimited time, usually in the form of a few extra minutes here or there. But she spoke for eight hours and ten minutes!

Pelosi was making a point. Her speech made history as the longest ever given on the floor. Wow, who can speak for eight hours straight?! Girl, according to the *Washington Post*'s reporting, "she barely took time to unwrap a mint several hours in." No food is allowed on the floor, just water. She had a tiny glass of water next to her. And she was standing in heels, ladies! For eight hours straight . . . speaking. Really, you have to wonder, is she Superwoman? "When's lunch?" would be even the strongest of people's response to such a task. But nope, she went straight on through. She barely looked up from her papers as she read the stories of DACA recipients as well as a few Bible verses. She was determined to make a stand and show the nation how hard she would fight.

THANKFULLY, SHE AND the rest of the House Democrats took that fight into the midterms later that year, and Pelosi overcame the GOP's efforts. After a tough two years in the minority under Trump, the House Democrats swept the 2018 midterms, winning back an impressive forty seats. Pelosi had a hand in that success, as she flexed her skills as the largest single fundraiser for the Democratic Congressional Campaign Committee. It was so much bigger than her, though: the 2018 election was one of the most exciting and diverse in history. Pelosi, as an OG, was excited about the changes that the new members would bring but also aware of the challenges of being a newbie.

When Queen of the Resistance Alexandria Ocasio-Cortez was running for Congress against longtime Democratic member Joe Crowley, according to her interview with *Time*, Pelosi called AOC from her office. "There's a lot to do," she said on that call. "Thank you for your courage to run. This is not for the faint of heart." Pelosi was brought up in Congress, and it was still a labor of love for her. Her dad had worn a bow tie decades before on the House floor, and she had grown up absorbing the worldview of social justice, JFK, and more than anything else moral obligation to her country. But it was hard work.

In fact, those new young members challenged her.

In the wake of the celebratory "blue wave" election, when it became clear that the next Speaker would be a Democrat, sixteen House Democrats signed a letter promising to vote *against* Pelosi for Speaker. **gasp** The letter said:

> *We are thankful to Leader Pelosi for her years of service to our Country and to our Caucus. She is a historic figure whose leadership has been instrumental to some of our party's most important legislative achievements. However, we also recognize that in this recent election, Democrats ran and won on a message of change. Our majority came on the backs of candidates who said that they would support new leadership because voters in hard-won districts, and across the country, want to see real change in Washington. We promised to change the status quo, and we intend to deliver on that promise.*

Of course, sixteen Dems were hardly a majority, sis; the entire House must vote for the election of Speaker. But if all sixteen of those Democratic members voted against Pelosi, and the House Republicans did too, she could possibly lose. She could try to get enough Republicans to vote for her to give her the kind of comfortable margin she was used to. But owing Republicans favors was not the kind of position she wanted to be in—remember, John Boehner had *quit Congress* rather than reach out to Pelosi to keep his own speakership. No, she knew she would have to cut a deal with the members of her caucus.

She could make the case that it wasn't the time to entertain a change of leadership—after all, they were in the midst of a political crisis. Though some may have agreed that change was needed and perhaps was inevitable, now did not seem to be the best time. There was no one else in the Democratic caucus who had the experience and skill to stand up to Donald Trump, especially if impeachment was required. They all knew it. Even Nancy knew it herself. She had to do something quick. Trump and the radicalized caucus he represented were going to be unpredictable and most likely unethical opponents. The situation required her cool head and political muscle.

She met with the sixteen opponents and was able to accept one of their key demands: term limits for Democratic House leadership. She had been the head of the Democratic caucus as either minority leader or Speaker since 2007. The rest of the Democratic leadership hadn't changed much over the past several years either. Young, talented Democrats had watched a group of young Republicans come up in the ranks of their party, while their own party remained the same. They wanted to be groomed for top spots, and new young members like Alexandria Ocasio-Cortez, Rashida Tlaib, and Ilhan Omar made it clear that they would not wait patiently.

Pelosi understood their concerns and agreed to limit her term as Speaker to another four years. After that, she would help usher in a new band of Democratic leaders in all the top spots.

"Over the summer, I made it clear that I see myself as a bridge to the next generation of leaders, a recognition of my continuing responsibility to mentor and advance new members into positions of power and responsibility in the House Democratic Caucus," Pelosi said in a statement. "I am comfortable with the proposal, and it is my intention to abide by it whether it passes or not."

In the end, the challengers were satisfied, and she coasted back to the Speaker's office, her votes of course counted well in advance.

IT WAS A good thing too: she got back to that seat just in time to put a stop to one of Trump's temper tantrums. *eye-roll* Here's the story: at the end of 2018, as the time to set the next year's federal budget approached, Trump had made it clear he expected the GOP-controlled Congress to get funding for his infamous border wall. (Remember, the House holds the purse strings. The president can make requests, but Congress does not need to respond to them.) And this president was determined to get his way by any means necessary.

The Democrats were against this, obviously, but many Republicans were also worried about putting funding in the budget for an impractical albatross of a border wall. All the facts showed that a border wall introduced new dangers that would only further complicate, not resolve, problems of immigration. So Trump signed an order a few days before Christmas to shut down the federal government in order to make an end run to get money for his border wall. *Oy!* The threat of a government shutdown was a pony Republicans had trotted out too many times since Newt Gingrich was Speaker.

Whenever the federal government shuts down, it's possible that Social Security recipients won't receive their checks, vendors won't be paid, and contractors who work for the federal government will never recoup their losses. Hundreds of thousands of government employees are sent home without pay, indefinitely. It has a reverberating effect that goes beyond the closing of museums, federal monuments, and the like, negatively affecting the lives of millions of people.

Pelosi called the action a "temper tantrum" because multiple proposals had been put forth to stop the shutdown, and Trump didn't care.

All of this was happening just weeks before Trump was due to give his 2019 State of the Union address to Congress. In order to do so, he must be formally invited by the Speaker of the House to come to the Hill to make the speech. As the shutdown dragged on, Pelosi disinvited Trump, saying that since the US Secret Service and the Department of Homeland Security were no longer getting paid, among other things, it would be unwise to move forward with the event until the shutdown was over. *Boo-yah!* With that bold, savvy move, Pelosi stood up to Trump and got her mojo back.

Newspapers applauded this showdown as a win for Pelosi and an embarrassment for Trump. He threatened to go to the House anyway, not realizing he had no authority to do so. Checkmate. Pelosi won that round.

On January 25, just four days before the planned State of the Union Address, Trump signed a stopgap resolution to re-open the government. He made his speech, and Pelosi delivered some extremely GIF-worthy applause behind him.

CHRONICLES OF AN IMPEACHMENT

The sun'll come out tomorrow.
Bet your bottom dollar that tomorrow there'll be sun.
—Annie, "Tomorrow"

The whole country, meanwhile, had been waiting for the Mueller Report to come out like kids anxiously awaiting the Easter Bunny or Santa Claus to appear, and in April it was released. It clearly demonstrated that the Russian government had interfered with the 2016 election in an unprecedented way, including involvement in the DNC server hack, and Mueller still had some questions about the Trump campaign's involvement. He had indicted, prosecuted, flipped, and even jailed top Trump campaign officials and cronies, including his campaign manager, Paul Manafort, and his personal lawyer, Michael Cohen. *Yikes!* Still, Mueller's report wasn't the smoking gun that the Democrats hoped it would be, and he sidestepped the whole issue of indicting a sitting president. Did he punk out? Or was he just a tad tired after writing a 448-page report?! In any case, he left it to Congress to decide what to do about Trump.

Always taking the long view, Pelosi had been skeptical of impeachment. Even though it was possible that this was one of the most problematic, if not corrupt, presidents in history, she worried about the political ramifications of impeaching him. She was concerned that if they went after this president who had such an unruly and volatile base, it might end in Democrats losing the momentum they had gained in 2018— if nothing else, the Dem-controlled House could be a check on harmful legislation.

Others, like the late Elijah Cummings, then chairman of the Committee on Oversight and Government Reform, and fellow Queen of the Resistance Maxine Waters, felt it was the responsibility of Congress to pursue these matters of potential criminal wrongdoing by the president, regardless of the cost, *okay*? And of course many Americans wanted to take out their fury with the president by way of an impeachment. How could politicians be upholding their oath to the Constitution, to protect against all enemies, foreign and domestic, if they let Trump get away with collusion with a foreign government?

Either way, the Mueller Report did not offer a clear opportunity to pursue the president without opening another investigation. So Pelosi allowed committees to do their work. She assigned several committees to be involved in this process— Ways and Means, Oversight and Reform, Judiciary, and Intelligence. They would all be involved in their own investigation and the gathering of information to determine whether Trump committed a crime.

While she did her job, the committees did theirs. First, the Ways and Means Committee tried to get ahold of the president's tax returns legally. It's not difficult to get the returns, but once they got them, they'd need to agree on how they could be shared to make a case for impeachment. If a citizen's private information is shared in the wrong way, even inadvertently, it can have serious legal consequences. But they wanted his tax returns to determine whether there was any economic incentive for Trump to be involved with the Russians. (Subsequently, it did come out that there was a question about a natural gas company that seemed to indicate what Trump hoped to gain from acting in concert with the Russian government. Just another scandal among the dozens, if not hundreds, of others . . .)

The committees also investigated whether Trump had violated the rules stating that the president cannot enrich himself while in office by leveraging the power of that office. There were some extremely questionable activities going on, including that the Trump hotel—which is just steps away, like, three blocks, from the White House—was a place where foreign governments and business owners would rent entire floors—though oddly no one would occupy them. Doing this amounted to putting money directly in the president's pocket.

While these investigations went on, as we now know, the president made some questionable (or, as he put it, "perfect") phone calls to the president of Ukraine, getting himself and the country into an entirely new mess. . . .

ON DECEMBER 18, 2019, the House of Representatives charged President Trump with abuse of power and obstruction of Congress. It turned out not to come from the Mueller investigation, but a new scandal altogether: an alleged scheme by the Trump administration, and possibly Trump himself, to pressure the president of Ukraine to investigate former Vice President Joe Biden, who by then was deep into the Democratic presidential primary campaign.

After thorough investigations, the House concluded that Trump had withheld $400 million in military assistance and used it as leverage in a telephone call with the Ukrainian president overheard by at least ten staffers and policy experts. This information on Biden would be used to bolster Trump's campaign, in an echo of what went down in the 2016 election. And, of course, he concealed this discussion from Congress.

To make matters worse, he also deployed his personal attorney, former NYC mayor Rudy Giuliani, as an outside consultant to press for the investigation he was seeking. The aid that Trump withheld ultimately served Russia's agenda in

Ukraine. Russia was fighting to take over territory in Ukraine, and the US dollars promised to Ukraine would have been used to bolster its military and keep the Russians out. It seemed no accident that Trump's plan also helped strengthen Russia's hand against Ukraine.

Pelosi did not jump for joy or run up and down the National Mall like you'd expect someone who had taken so much of a butt-kicking from people who thought that she was being a wuss not to impeach after the Mueller investigation. Reporters noticed her somber attire: she wore a dark suit and a brooch of the Mace of the Republic, a symbol of the House. She had to be appropriately serious, not self-satisfied like we wanted, sis. It brought out mixed feelings among the American people who despised Trump for his misogynist, racist, xenophobic acts and politics, who had endured *years* of traumatizing *daily* news flashes. They'd suffered breakups with loved ones, estrangement from their Trump-supporting family members, tears for their Muslim, immigrant, and minority brothers and sisters; it was a freakin' emotional roller coaster. Oddly, the "impeachment party" they were looking for turned out to be more like an impeachment funeral. "Our founders' vision of a republic is under threat from actions from the White House. That is why today, as Speaker of the House, I solemnly and sadly open the debate on the impeachment of the president of the United States," she said. There were no kegs, Jell-O shots, or party streamers. Nope, girlfriend, that's

not Pelosi's style. The need for an impeachment wasn't something to celebrate. It was, in fact, tragic.

It was shocking to Trump, to say the least. He spent that Christmas having a Twitter tantrum.

> Why should Crazy Nancy Pelosi, just because
> she has a slight majority in the House, be
> allowed to Impeach the President of the United
> States? Got Zero Republican votes, there was
> no crime, the call with Ukraine was perfect, with
> "no pressure."

Totally normal thing for a president to announce publicly, let alone on Christmas Day. Let's see how Pelosi's public statements on him compare, shall we?

Only a few weeks earlier, at a December 5 news conference, a journalist named James Rosen, of the conservative Sinclair Broadcast Group, asked Pelosi if she hated the president as she was walking out. She did a U-turn back to the mic to put him and anyone else who had the same obnoxious question in their place. "I think this president is a coward when it comes to helping our kids who are afraid of gun violence. I think he is cruel when he doesn't deal with helping our Dreamers, of which we are very proud. I think he's in denial about the climate crisis.

"However," she said, swerving her neck, "that's about the

election. Take it up in the election. This is about the Constitution of the United States and the facts that lead to the president's violation of his oath of office. And as a Catholic, I resent your using the word 'hate' in a sentence that addresses me. I don't hate anyone. I was raised [to have] a heart full of love and always pray for the president. And I still pray for the president. I pray for the president all the time. So don't mess with me when it comes to words like that."

It was a classic Pelosi clapback: she laid down the facts, dragged the president for his track record, and took the high road while letting us enjoy the low-key shade. Girl, you can't do much better than "I pray for the president all the time." Ha!

For Pelosi, the impeachment of the president wasn't a cause for celebration or backslapping. Holding the president accountable is an important duty in the House, and the Speaker took that duty very seriously. In her announcement on December 18, she took an almost spiritual tone. "In signing the Declaration of Independence, our founders invoked a firm reliance on divine providence. Democrats too are prayerful, and we will proceed in a manner worthy of our oath of office to support and defend the Constitution of the United States from all enemies, foreign and domestic, so help us God."

On January 10, 2020, Pelosi announced that she would appoint members to deliver to the Senate charges of abuse of power and obstruction of Congress. In her letter, Madam

Speaker wrote, "In an impeachment trial, every senator takes an oath to 'do impartial justice according to the Constitution and laws.' Every senator now faces a choice: to be loyal to the president or the Constitution." After she signed the articles of impeachment, she handed them to House Clerk Cheryl Johnson, who began a solemn procession to deliver them by hand to the Senate chamber. Johnson walked through the halls alongside the seven impeachment managers Pelosi had named, those who had played major roles in the investigations and hearings that led to this moment. It was out of her hands now, literally. Her impeachment work was done.

No matter what else happens to Donald Trump, from that day forward, he would forever be labeled as an impeached president. Even with the naysayers breathing down her neck, Pelosi did it her way. She made her moves cleverly and effectively. True to form, she counted her votes, even when the odds seemed stacked against her and her caucus. She came at the man who would love to be king, and she *did not miss*.

★

EPILOGUE

You didn't think we were going to end this story with a focus on *Donald Trump*, did you? Ha! No.

Let's backtrack for a moment to January 3, 2019, the day that Speaker Pelosi had the pleasure of swearing in new members of Congress—many of them members who made up the new Democratic majority. So many moments, and a monumental effort, had led up to that joyful day. From an explosion in grassroots campaigning to new candidates who had never run before—especially women—and an intense dedication by then Minority Leader Pelosi's caucus to slowing or stopping as many pieces of harmful legislation as possible, came the bright new dawn of the 116th Congress.

Taking back the majority was plenty of reason to celebrate, but it wasn't the only thing for Pelosi to feel proud of. In the nearly thirty-two years since she first entered Congress, the chamber had transformed from an almost total boys' club (and an overwhelmingly white one, at that) to the most diverse representation the House has ever seen. Twenty-five other women served alongside freshman member Pelosi in 1987; on that day in 2019, eighty-seven women were part of her caucus alone. *snap. snap.*

In short, we've come a long way, baby. And Madam Speaker knows it. In the run-up to that historic day of swearing in the new Congress, remember, Pelosi promised the new wave of Democrats that she would only lead the party in the House for four more years. She knows it's just about time to pass the baton to a worthy new generation of leaders; after her historic achievements as Speaker, she will leave an impressive legacy for the next school to build upon. She's modeled in so many ways the path to doing it *right*: playing the long game for her caucus, forging connections with friends and potential rivals alike, and always counting her votes.

After centuries of male control of the gavel, Madam Speaker's tenure has shown us that she was more than ready for the job—she will go down in history as one of the most effective Speakers, and she did it by wielding a distinctly feminine type of power. And that might just be the best part of Speaker Pelosi's legacy: there's no doubt that future women leaders are growing up knowing *exactly* what's possible.

BRENDA JONES and KRISHAN TROTMAN

ACKNOWLEDGMENTS

Our agent, Johanna Castillo, at Writers House is a true queen of the resistance and must go at the top of our acknowledgments. Wow, she is the very definition of love, creativity, and strength. We absolutely would not have had this opportunity without her strong vision and ability to keep us in check to get it done. We adore and honor you, queen. You are a changemaker who made our lifelong dreams of being published authors come true. Anytime you call us to have tea in your kitchen, we'll be there ASAP.

Thank you to the wonderful team at Plume who believed in this four-book series to celebrate these Queens of the Resistance. Special acknowledgments, high fives, dabs, and e-hugs to our brilliant, kind, and badass queen editors, Jill Schwartzman and Marya Pasciuto, and to the Plume team, who kept up the strong sisterhood and encouragement through and through to get this project done! *Yes, we can!* Thank you to the queens: Amanda Walker, Jamie Knapp, Becky Odell, Katie Taylor, Caroline Payne, Leila Siddiqui, Tiffany Estreicher, Alice Dalrymple, LeeAnn Pemberton, Susan Schwartz, Kaitlin Kall, and Dora Mak—and there were two good-guy allies who need a special shout-out, the editor in chief, John Parsley, and the creative director, Christopher Lin. To our publisher, Christine Ball, a strong woman and leader from the moment we met her, we especially love the army you've built and the work that you continue to innovate. Thank you!

THANK YOU, THANK YOU, THANK YOU (in all caps) to our beloved Ava Williams, our research assistant. You didn't know what you were getting yourself into, lol, but your positive vibes and hard work held it up the entire time from beginning to end. Thank you for your warm and patient spirit throughout the process.

THANK YOU, THANK YOU, THANK YOU (in all caps) to the talented Jonell Joshua for your beautiful images and being a creative who could make it through all the deadlines with precision. You're the best, girlfriend!

Krishan would like to give a big shout-out to her personal sister circle, the women in her life who took the lead in helping with Bleu on those daylong playdates: my sister, Dominique Marie Bell, Raven Brown-Walters, Renee Brown-Walters, Lenica Gomez, Zaira Vasco. Special thanks to my crew at WeInspire—JLove, Brea Baker, and Taylor Shaw—and also to my mentors who guide me, especially Adrienne Ingrum, who has been a wonderful fountain of knowledge and inspiration throughout my path. This is for my mom, a queen of the resistance from Brooklyn and the Bronx, New York, who left us too soon but whom I felt watching over me from heaven smiling; and her twin, my loving auntie Amina Samad, who always came over with love and hugs to help throughout the process—I love and cherish you both so very much. Thank you to my son, Xavier Bleu Jeune, for being such an awesome growing boy. I love being #BleusMom. My favorite moment in this journey was when you said you wanted to be a "comedic author" (not to be confused with author, *okay*). I love you. And last but never least, thank you to my copilot, Brenda, for rockin' this out with me!

Brenda would like to thank her friends on Capitol Hill; without your passion and determination to fight legislatively and strategically in this hard time, our democracy might no longer exist. My struggle for you here was to incline this project toward a true representation of your sacrifice, intellect, and capability. To special friends who helped me hang in there: Kathryn Williams, Cheryl Johnson, Shashrina Thomas, Ingrid Gavin-Parks, Kim Ross, Michael Hagbourne, Joan Kelsey, and the DMV Quartet. Thanks to Bernard Demczuk for opening the Growlery at Giverny West whenever I needed quiet concentration. To the absolute best parents—the late

Myrtle Bowers Davis and Robert Lee Davis—who instilled in me the highest integrity, the best education, and the richest experiences. To Rep. John Lewis, without whom my career in politics would never have been possible. Thank you for your unwavering faith in me and unyielding commitment to art, inspiration, creativity, justice, and peace.

Thanks to Speaker Nancy Pelosi, Chairwoman Maxine Waters, Sen. Elizabeth Warren, and Rep. Alexandria Ocasio-Cortez for your bright shining lives of public service. Krishan, Plume, and I can only hope that we have begun to return to you just a small part of what you sacrifice so much to give to us all. Hail the Queens of the Resistance.

To our readers, from our hearts to yours, *thank you*, *thank you*, *thank you* for celebrating the Queens of the Resistance series with us!

SOURCES

Archdiocese of Baltimore. "Catholic Legislators Must Protect Life, Pope Tells Speaker Pelosi." Archbalt.org, January 19, 2012.

Barabak, Mark Z. "Times Profile: Nancy Pelosi." *Los Angeles Times*, January 26, 2003.

Beinart, Peter. "The Nancy Pelosi Problem." *The Atlantic*, April 2018.

Bess, Levin. "Pelosi Accuses Facebook Execs of Being Misogynistic A-Holes." *Vanity Fair*, May 29, 2019.

C-SPAN. "Election of Nancy Pelosi as Speaker of the House." January 4, 2007.

Cargle, Rachel Elizabeth. "Why You Need to Stop Saying, 'All Lives Matter.'" *Harper's Bazaar*, April 16, 2019.

Clift, Eleanor. "Fast Chat: NANCY PELOSI." *Newsweek*, December 30, 2002.

Clymer, Adam. "Woman in the News; A New Vote Counter—Nancy Patricia Pelosi." *The New York Times*, October 11, 2001.

CNN. "Nancy Pelosi Fast Facts." CNN.com, October 8, 2019.

Cohen, Richard E. "In Her Own Words: Nancy Pelosi." *National Journal*, May 7, 2010.

Congresswoman Nancy Pelosi, California's 12th District. "Education." Accessed February 4, 2020, https://pelosi.house.gov/issues/education.

———. "Full Biography." Accessed February 4, 2020, https://pelosi.house.gov/biography-0.

———. "Housing." Accessed February 4, 2020, https://pelosi.house.gov/issues/housing.

———. "Human Rights." Accessed February 4, 2020, https://pelosi.house.gov/issues/human-rights.

———. "Internet Freedom." Accessed February 4, 2020, https://pelosi.house.gov/issues/internet-freedom.

———. "Jobs and Economic Justice." Accessed February 4, 2020, https://pelosi.house.gov/issues/jobs-and-economic-justice.

———. "LGBTQ." Accessed February 4, 2020, https://pelosi.house.gov/issues/lgbtq.

———. "National Security." Accessed February 4, 2020, https://pelosi.house.gov/issues/national-security.

———. "Over 30 Years of Results for San Francisco." Accessed February 4, 2020, https://pelosi.house.gov/biography/over-30-years-of-results-for-san-francisco.

———. "Pelosi Statement on House Filing Amicus Brief in Lawsuit Against Trump." Accessed February 4, 2020, https://pelosi.house.gov/news/press-releases/pelosi-statement-on-housefiling-amicus-brief-in-lawsuit-against-trump-s-junk.

———. "Pelosi Statement on Republicans' War on Women's Rights and Health." Press release. Pelosi.house.gov, January 24, 2017, https://pelosi.house.gov/news/press-releases/pelosi-statement-on-republicans-war-on-women-s-rights-and-health.

———. "Retirement Security." Accessed February 4, 2020, https://pelosi.house.gov/issues/retirement-security.

———. "Women's Economic Agenda." Accessed February 4, 2020, https://pelosi.house.gov/issues/womens-economic-agenda.

Cottle, Michelle. "House Broker." *The New Republic*, June 11, 2008, https://newrepublic.com/article/62262/house-broker.

Currinder, Marian. "Nancy Pelosi and Steny Hoyer: How Their Past Rivalry Helped Shape the Future of Leadership Races." Legbranch.org, May 3, 2018.

Davis, Julie Hirschfeld. "Tensions Between Pelosi and Progressive Democrats of 'The Squad' Burst into Flame." *The New York Times*, July 9, 2019.

Donadio, Rachel. "Visiting Pope, Pelosi Hears a Call to Protect Life." *The New York Times*, February 18, 2009.

Dowd, Maureen. "Nancy Pelosi Spanks the First Brat." *The New York Times*, January 12, 2019.

———. "Why Is Nancy Pelosi Praying for Trump?" *Harper's Bazaar*, October 1, 2019.

Eilperin, Juliet. "Democrats Pick Pelosi as House Whip." *The Washington Post*, October 11, 2001.

Epstein, Edward. "Pelosi Becomes Madam Speaker." *San Francisco Chronicle*, January 4, 2007.

———. "Pelosi Proud of Dems' Work in First 100 Days: Speaker Given High Marks for Keeping 233 Diverse Members of Her Party in Line on Tough Votes by Leading from the Center." *San Francisco Chronicle*, March 29, 2007.

Ferraro, Thomas. "Pelosi Becomes First Woman to Lead House." Reuters, January 21, 2007.

Ferraro, Thomas, and Rachelle Younglai. "House Chooses Boehner as Speaker Again Despite Dissent." Reuters, January 3, 2013.

Harmon, Andrew. "The World According to Nancy Pelosi." *Advocate*, February 2012.

Harris, Gardiner. "President Obama and Nancy Pelosi Share Stage After Setback." *The New York Times*, June 19, 2015, https://www.nytimes.com/2015/06/20/us/politics/obama-and-nancy-pelosi-share-stage-after-setback.html.

Hickey, Walt, Mariana Alfaro, and Grace Panetta. "Today Is Nancy Pelosi's 79th Birthday—Here's How She Went from San Francisco Housewife to the Most Powerful Woman in US Politics." *Business Insider*, March 26, 2019.

History, Art, and Archives, United States House of Representatives. "Burton, Sala Galante." Accessed February 4, 2020, https://history.house.gov/People/Detail/10266.

Icsman, Marilyn. "Pelosi Donates Speaker's Gavel to Smithsonian." *USA Today*, March 7, 2018.

Kang, Cecilia. "Nancy Pelosi Criticizes Facebook for Handling of Altered Videos." *The New York Times*, May 29, 2019.

Kapur, Sahil. "Nancy Pelosi Is Worried 2020 Candidates Are on Wrong Track." Bloomberg.com, November 2, 2019.

Kelley, Makena. "House Speaker Nancy Pelosi Says It's Time to Regulate Big Tech." *The Verge*, June 4, 2019.

Kragie, Andrew. "The Democrats Who Adored George H. W. Bush." *The Atlantic*, December 1, 2018.

Lim, Naomi. "'Dems Divided': Nancy Pelosi at Odds with Maxine Waters over Impeachment." *Washington Examiner*, April 23, 2019.

Lollar, Chelsea. "Nancy Pelosi Is About Her Job—And America's Future." *Junior Scholastic*, March 12, 2007.

Love, Keith. "Special Election Will Be Set for S.F.'s 5th District." *Los Angeles Times*, February 3, 1987.

Love, Keith, and Dan Morain. "Pelosi Wins Democratic Contest for Burton Seat." *Los Angeles Times*, April 8, 1987.

Mayer, Jane. "Power Walk." *The New Yorker*, November 14, 2011.

Mervosh, Sarah. "Distorted Videos of Nancy Pelosi Spread on Facebook and Twitter, Helped by Trump." *The New York Times*, May 24, 2019.

Montanaro, David. "Nancy Pelosi on Bill Clinton's Impeachment in 1998: Republicans Are Paralyzed with Hatred." Fox News, September 25, 2019.

Morin, Rebecca. "Black Female Leaders Criticize Pelosi, Schumer for 'Failure to Protect' Waters." *Politico*, July 4, 2018.

Newton-Small, Jay. "6 Questions with Nancy Pelosi." *Time*, December 12, 2015.

Nguyen, Tina. "How Nancy Pelosi Humiliated Trump on Infrastructure Week." *Vanity Fair*, May 22, 2019, https://www.vanityfair.com/news/2019/05/donald-trump-nancy-pelosi-infrastructure-deal.

Nilsen, Ella. "Pelosi Learned the Art of 'No' from Working with Bush. Trump Is a Whole New Test." *Vox*, January 18, 2019.

On the Issues. "Nancy Pelosi in State of the Union Address." Ontheissues.org. Accessed February 18, 2020.

Padilla, Mariel, and Mihir Zaveri. "Thomas D'Alesandro, 90, Ex-Mayor of Baltimore and Pelosi's Brother, Dies." *The New York Times*, October 22, 2019.

Peller, Lauren. "Nancy Pelosi Doesn't Like the Idea of Impeachment or Medicare for All." CBS News, November 1, 2019.

Pelosi, Nancy. Speaker of the House. "About." Accessed February 4, 2020, https://www.speaker.gov/about.

———. "Nancy Pelosi: Floor Speech on Reid Debt Limit Bill." July 30, 2011.

———. "Pelosi Commencement Address to the Class of 2016 Graduates at Morgan State University." May 2016.

———. "Pelosi Commencement Address at San Francisco State University." 2019.

———. "Pope Talks to Pelosi on Abortion." Associated Press, streamed live on February 18, 2009, YouTube video, 1:08, https://www.youtube.com/watch?v=4Z0wezHBvyY.

———. "Speaker Pelosi Biography." Accessed February 4, 2020, https://www.speaker.gov/sites/speaker.house.gov/files/documents/Speaker-Pelosi-Biography.pdf.

Pelosi, Nancy, with Amy Bill Hearth. *Know Your Power*. New York: Anchor Books, 2009.

Prokop, Andrew. "In 2005, Republicans Controlled Washington. Their Agenda Failed. Here's Why." *Vox*, January 9, 2017.

Sandalow, Marc. *Madam Speaker*. New York: Rodale Press, 2008.

Schiro, Anne-Marie. "Host Committee Is Led by a 'Natural' Organizer." *The New York Times*, July 17, 1984.

Sorokko, Tatiana. "Nancy Pelosi Speaks Her Mind." *Harper's Bazaar*, July 16, 2008, https://www.harpersbazaar.com/culture/features/a317/nancy-pelosi-interview-0808/.

Steinhauer, Jennifer. "In Pelosi, Strong Catholic Faith and Abortion Rights Coexist." *The New York Times*, September 21, 2015.

Time. "'It's Always About Mom.' Nancy Pelosi Praises Her Mother at the TIME 100 Gala." April 24, 2019.

Waweru, James. "The Untold Truth of Nancy Pelosi's Husband, Paul Pelosi." Thenetline.com, August 27, 2019.

Yglesias, Matthew. "The Time Nancy Pelosi Saved Social Security." *Vox*, November 21, 2018.

Zernike, Kate. "Nancy Pelosi: Demonized or Celebrated, She Refuses to Agonize." *The New York Times*, November 4, 2018.

ABOUT THE AUTHORS

Brenda Jones is best known for her fifteen-year tenure as communications director for an icon of American politics, Rep. John Lewis. All of his published opinions, statements, and speeches, ranging from his introductions of US presidents to commencement addresses delivered to the Ivy League, and those celebrating his transformative Civil Rights legacy were penned by Brenda Jones during that time. She collaborated with him on his book, *Across That Bridge: A Vision for Change and the Future of America*, which won an NAACP Image Award. She has also worked in commercial television news and public broadcasting.

Krishan Trotman is an executive editor at Hachette Books, recently profiled in *Essence* magazine as one of the few African American publishing executives. She has committed more than fifteen years to publishing books by and about multicultural voices and social justice. Throughout her career as an editor she has proudly worked with leaders and trail-blazers on this frontier, such as John Lewis, Stephanie Land, Malcolm Nance, Zerlina Maxwell, Mika Brzezinski, Al Roker, Ryan Serhant, and Lindy West.